BEYOND
Bodegas

OTHER MARKETING BOOKS FROM PMP

The Kids Market: *Myths & Realities*

The Great Tween Buying Machine

Marketing to American Latinos, Part I

Marketing to American Latinos, Part II

The Mirrored Window: *Focus Groups
from a Moderator's Point of View*

Moderating to the Max! *A Full-tilt Guide to Creative
Focus Groups and Insightful Depth Interviews*

Marketing Insights to Help Your Business Grow

Why People Buy Things They Don't Need

A Knight's Code of Business: *How to Achieve
Character and Competence in the Corporate World*

India Business: *Finding Opportunities
in this Big Emerging Market*

After Fifty: *How the Baby Boom Will
Redefine the Mature Market*

The Whole Enchilada: *Hispanic Marketing 101*

BEYOND
Bodegas

Developing a Retail Relationship with Hispanic Customers

Jim Perkins

PARAMOUNT MARKET PUBLISHING, INC.

Paramount Market Publishing, Inc.
301 S. Geneva Street, Suite 109
Ithaca, NY 14850
www.paramountbooks.com
Telephone: 607-275-8100; 888-787-8100   Facsimile: 607-275-8101

Publisher: James Madden
Editorial Director: Doris Walsh

Cataloging in Publication Data available
ISBN 0-9725290-3-9

Book design and composition: Paperwork

Contents

3995

115703

Dedication

For my late father whose name, good deeds, and daily pursuit of knowledge remain eternal in me. At my departure gate for my first academic trip to Spain, he jubilantly stated, "My son, your odyssey is about to begin." Really Dad, it began when you suggested I study Spanish when I was 10!

For my mother for her unique blend of determination, faith, hope, and unconditional support! You invoke kindness and practice generosity. I am never more proud when I say, "This is my Mom! This is my beautiful Mom."

Ever an inspiration, thank you both for instilling in me the ability to think differently and to recognize the profound beauty of knowledge, life, and love.

Acknowledgements

Can you help me better understand? These have been the words I have said so many times to so many wonderful and brilliant people. The research for this book was pleasurable. It allowed me to travel to distant lands, back to the classroom, into and out on the streets and markets of Olvera in Los Angeles, Las Ramblas in Barcelona and La Reforma in México City and to the open air vegetable markets of Tarragona, Spain, China Town in San Francisco and Chicago. It should be easy to understand how blessed I am.

Like a symphony, many musicians work in harmony to produce a perfect sound. To the many who have contributed and worked in harmony with me to produce this book, I applaud you all.

Cindy Rae, your patience and support, strength and various journeys to numerous Latin markets have contributed immensely. You are the attention to detail in this book.

Dr. Raymond Merritt and your countless news clippings and academic insight to numerous portions of this book, I thank you!

Jim Madden, the publisher, Jim's favorite words to me, "The first 40 percent of what most people write are mere words and the last 10 percent is the most difficult." I can't disagree. Doris Walsh, the editor, coach, teacher. Your steadfast desire to help me better write an entertaining and informative book has encouraged me to do so.

I have been the pupil of many.

Luis Chapa and the Chapa Family of 7-Eleven of México. Thanks for the opportunity to join a wonderful family and to learn from the best operators and merchandisers of convenience stores I have worked with in North America. Your support and 'amistad' don't go unnoticed.

Bruce McAllaster of the Southland Corporation. You fortified and further developed my ability to be a servant leader and helped me manage others while recognizing the role faith plays in all relationships.

Brad Burmaster, your management style fits and from you I have learned that how hard a person tries should be recognized.

Gary Dawson, thanks for completing the research with me over a soccer match and a bullfight in Guadalajara, México; you ask the questions others don't think to ask or don't have the courage to ask. You are my talented friend!

Adrianna Correa, *mil gracias* for saying, "I am Mexican and I did not know that!" You have contributed so very much to the process of this book and to the cultural insights presented in this book. *Mí amiga—Amigos para siempre.*

Jorge at Café Baba Reba in Chicago. How much time have we shared with me asking you questions about life here and in Mexico? Comparing and contrasting? You mix great sangria my amigo! *¡Encantado de conocerte, el placer es mio!*

Thanks to Guillermo Guarino and his life perspective and the life he and his family share with me in San Diego. Thank you for adding love to my life! You are my fifth brother. My Latin brother!

Every person who wants to learn about how to build brand-level communications at t he retail level should meet Debra Núñez McWhirter. Her friendly attitude, generous personality, and dedication to this consumer don't go unnoticed.

Martha de la Vega at La Villita Chamber of Commerce, your contribution to this book is immense; however it is second to what you do for your community. You should be proud of your work, I certainly am!

François Fournier at the MFM Group, The lessons I have learned from your seminars are lifelong and pieces of them are found within the pages of this book!

Dennis de la Mata—Big D. How does a guy from Brooklyn who is Cuban and Spanish arrive in Chicago, keep parts of the Brooklyn demeanor, become a wine collector, fine chef and baseball know it all? You are a study in acculturation my friend. The journey has been tremendous. Have you ever thought that when you don't make it home on time after *béisbol* games, it could just be the Latino in you?

To the special people at the National Pork Board, Hallmark Cards, The Packer Fresh Trends, Coca-Cola, WLEY in Chicago, Nissan Motors in Los Angeles, Coca-Cola México, Oxxo de México, Petroleos de Venezuela S.A., the University of California at Berkeley, Gigante de México, Carre Four, numerous chambers of commerce, the Produce Marketing Association, The Food Marketing Institute, Arandas Tires and my classmates— you all have contributed significantly to the understanding of this powerful consumer base.

Fr. John Hoffman of St. Teresa of Avila, Chicago. For the space to write the book.

Fr. Mark Pranaitis of Saint Vincent DePaul, Chicago. Your thoughts and comments make me a better thinker

My family: We are seven kids and we are family. Your love, support, and encouragement of me has been with me since I was brought into your world. Thanks for being very different and unique siblings to me, each offering to me unconditionally.

To my brother, Rev. Nicholas Perkins CSP, who is as important to me as the daily rising sun. Thanks for the steadfast support, the late night conversations from all over the world, and the ever-present guidance across the course of my life. I am fortunate to refer to you as MY brother and I am in awe of YOUR life accomplishments.

And to my Uncle Tello, simply the definition of cool! You have helped teach me about life and it shows in the research for this book!

Retail's Life Lessons

On April 29, 1992 I was on a special assignment for Mobil Oil Corporation with an older and wiser co-worker, Ralph Ripke. Our task was to share the concept of Total Quality Management with retailers, service station owners, vendors, contractors, and Mobil management and to provide ideas, concepts and practices for improving our business by addressing issues related to diversity. On that day, we were in a classroom in San Luis Obispo, California. It was a beautiful spot, even if the classroom for this event was in the back room of a service station. In the late afternoon we heard about the rioting mobs igniting fires in Los Angeles, some 200 miles to our south. I remember Ralph's words, "Jim, Los Angeles is coming apart. I think we best find our way back to LA." That night and many nights to follow, all residents of Los Angeles were under curfew, ordered to remain in their homes.

You may wonder why I would start a book on retailing and Hispanic consumers by recalling the 1992 Los Angeles riots, which erupted when the jury in the televised trial of the four officers accused in the beating of Rodney King announced they had found the officers innocent. For years to come, sociologists will attempt to find out why this happened. What were the deep roots that ignited this tragedy, this rebellion? There will be many questions and many answers. However, there was really only one direct, immediate cause that was the flash point—the verdict.

Death, destruction of countless retail establishments, race problems, and poor relations with city government topped the list of the aftermath of the LA riots. In all there was a breakdown of civility as we know it. Throughout a city seething with smoke was a city seething about race relations. However, in the midst of the widespread looting and destruction, some gas stations, mom and pop stores, supermarkets, appliance stores, and dry cleaners in the riot torn areas surrounding Florence and Normandie, were not destroyed—not even touched. Quite the contrary! These retailers were open for business, perhaps not during the riots, but certainly afterward.

In the post-riot days in Los Angeles, I drove through the embattled area of South Central Los Angeles. What amazed me was the lack of damage to one convenience store directly across the street from one that was looted and burned.

To better understand why one business survived while another did not is to better understand the relationship between community, marketing and retail, and survival. For some, survival meant taking up arms, standing at the entryways or perching on the rooftops to protect their businesses. For other businesses, protection and the insulation from this catastrophic civil unrest was initiated when these businesspeople first moved into the neighborhood or *barrio* or Korea Town and decided to be part of the community.

They decided to sell products that the community wanted.

They decided to advertise and market and speak in the language of the community.

They decided to sponsor Little League teams and buy Girl Scout cookies as active members of the community.

They decided to allow neighborhood lunch wagons with Latin food to park in their lots to provide food for the members of their employed community during lunch.

Owners pleaded nervously with looters not to take from the store and therefore take from the community. They asked them not to pilfer and destroy a place of employment for the community that hired Juan after high school and gave a retired Ana the afternoon shift for extra income to help feed her grandchildren or a mom a part time job!

How they survived

I spoke to numerous survivors. They credited their hiring practices with survival. Their employees lived, looked, spoke, and danced like those in South Central Los Angeles. They had good employees, smart employees. In exchange the employees were given opportunity, responsibility, honor, health plans, and a way of life.

As for the ones that didn't survive, especially the franchises that populated this landscape, perhaps the destruction to their location was simply a random act of evil, a mob action. Or, perhaps a contributing factor was not recognizing and participating in the community in which they were operating.

So, I open this book on attracting Hispanic consumers to your place of business with a lesson from the 1992 riots of Los Angeles because the book is about experiences and practices that will help you understand how to win the hearts and minds of your Hispanic customers.

The Los Angeles riot is but one example. In major cities like Chicago, Miami, Seville, Spain, Caracas, Venezuela, Monterrey, Mexico and Mexico City as well as smaller places like Prairie du Sac, Wisconsin and Imperial Beach, California I have come to better understand what it is that people want when they are away from their homes. Product selection, environment, name recognition, color, and language—what I call retail "content." When I travel outside the United States, I want to feel wanted, to feel accepted, to feel comfortable with my surroundings, in essence to feel as if I can contribute. It is no different for Latinos who make their way to the United States.

It is through travel and my passion for the Spanish language and culture that I have gained an understanding of how homeland culture and retail content and marketing influence the purchasing decisions of those who come to this country from other countries. It is because of travel and friends who are Latino and Hispanic that I have come to better understand what and who drives the purchase decision.

And it is because of travel, friends, my parents, and my education that I have the opportunity to share with you now my take not only on how to market and attract Hispanics to your place of business, but also how to enjoy the uniqueness of this colorful, vibrant and financially stable consumer.

Blame it on my dad

Rick Bayless, a popular, successful, and acclaimed chef, restaurant owner and author, was once asked, "How is a guy with the last name of Bayless able to build one of the most successful Mexican restaurants and brands in the country?" Bayless answered, "I have been back and forth to Mexico many times, searching for the proper spices and the proper culture for my food and restaurant. I feel and have always felt like my inner spirit lives in Mexico. Mexico and food are my passion."

How is a guy with the last name of Perkins able to write a book on retail and the U.S. Hispanic? My transformation began in the sixth grade when I had to take a foreign language. I decided to take French, but first I was told to discuss it with my parents—a Polish mom and a Welsh dad. Before the F of French broke the seal of my lips my dad said, "Change that to Spanish —tomorrow!"

It was in that Spanish class I learned the first lesson in life that many retailers struggle with today—judging the book by its cover! During Spanish class with Señora Topete, we arrived at the vocabulary lesson of the day and the words contained the letter R, the Spanish R.

There I sat, nervously waiting to be called upon to repeat *ahora* or *carro* or some other word with R. Finally, it was my turn to anguish through the words. Seriously, during the second and third grades I went to speech therapy to correct the lazy R in English, so how, four years later could I pronounce *ahora* and *carro?* The words came and passed and so did my embarrassment. I regained composure, and listened for pretty Cristina sitting behind me to pronounce the words. No sweat for her I thought. Her deep brown eyes and jet black hair seemed a perfect match for the Spanish R. Her pronunciation sounded only slightly better than mine; it was not like Señora Topete's. So much for judging the book by its cover. Cristina was much less "Spanish gifted" than I had assumed, but she, along with the Del Rio boys from my neighborhood were my introduction to Latin culture. Cristina and I graduated from middle school and attended the same high school. She invited me to my first *quinceañera*, or her fifteenth birthday, a celebration of faith, religion, and the arrival to womanhood that has its roots in Mexico, perhaps with the Aztecs.

My love for Spanish and diversity has been with me since my youth. I lived in an ethnic neighborhood. Within one mile we had seven different churches. Within one block we had the Nottoli, Del Rio, Mitchell, Wickhurst, Madura, Muholland, Panapolous, Iatridies, McCarthy and the Karras families. It was a world full of life, where Orthodox Jews were seen walking to synagogue on Saturday afternoon, and Sundays were spent taking food to your neighbors, just because.

Like Mr. Bayless, my inner being is most comfortable when traveling to Mexico, Spain, Los Angeles, or Miami. My best Sundays include the 10:30 a.m. Mass at St. Teresa of Avila in Lincoln Park, Chicago with Puerto Ricans. In Old Town San Diego, with my friend Guillermo, my soul is stirred and my Spanish energized and it is at Café Ba Ba Reba with my favorite *cantinero* (bartender) Jorge that we pass time discussing the goodness of life.

It is with this energy that I write this book. The same energy and courage it took to pronounce Spanish R, eat *Cabrito* in Mexico and travel to Madrid from Seville via train for the Grad School Examination only to discover the address for the test did not exist.

The lessons of my earlier life act as a foundation for the lessons realized in later life. The ability to embrace all people from all traditions is celebrating life as well as diversity. The constant awareness of our identity and the identity of others depends on communication and sharing and the self-discipline to listen and accept and when appropriate, respectfully challenge and inquire.

This is indeed a book about marketing to Hispanics, but it is full of non-corporate lessons that are part of my past and part of a mission. We (you, the reader, and me, the writer) are commissioned—to go forward (missioned) together (co). In my neighborhood as a child, we depended on each other. When the river overflowed and homes were in danger, we were commissioned or sent forward to work together to save our homes.

In business, Ford or Pepsi, Visa or Sears, 7-Eleven or the local Panaderia, we depend on each other because without each other we will not move forward.

So, to begin, ask yourself, "Do I have good dirt? Good practical real estate?" Have you built something that is commissioned for the community in which you operate? Do people return? Is it good land? Is it rich? Is it fertile? Friendly? Staffed properly? Clean? Regardless of whether you are associated with groceries, restaurants, e-commerce, publishing, insurance, health care, manufacturing, education, or city government, this should be your first concern. If you have good dirt and provide a service or product for the community, your customers will return! And together moving forward you, your business, and the citizens of your community will flourish and be satisfied.

May this book assist all who read it in their quest to cultivate community and build rich dirt!

JIM PERKINS
CHICAGO, 2004

CHAPTER 1

Why Hispanics, Why Now?

By now everyone in marketing and sales knows that the fastest-growing ethnic group in the United States is Hispanic. What you may not know is that Hispanic buying power is also taking off and expected to reach more than $1 trillion by 2008, according to projections by the Selig Center at the University of Georgia.

Why is Hispanic buying power growing?

One factor is sheer numbers of people. The Hispanic population continues to grow through immigration and fertility rates that are higher than those in non-Hispanic households. The most recent Current Population Survey (March 2002) shows that more than one of every eight people in the United States considers him or herself Hispanic. In 2002, there were 37.4 million documented Hispanics in the United States (not including Puerto Rico), representing 13.3 percent of the total population overall. In the West however, Hispanics are 44.2 percent of the population, making them a clear "majority minority." In the South, they are 34.8 percent of the population, a slightly higher percentage of the population than non-Hispanic whites.

Second, Hispanics have better employment opportunities in this country than ever before. Many who were young professionals in the late 1980s and early 1990s are moving up the career ladder, especially as companies recognize that they may have special insights to offer firms who are trying to appeal to Hispanic customers. Others are moving beyond the "diversity' jobs into general management.

Third, there is a strong entrepreneurial tendency among Hispanics, many of whom have capital, family support, and courage enough to open their own businesses. Many of these businesses have been stalwarts of their communities for years. Others are just breaking in. Some of these businesses serve Hispanic neighborhoods, but many like the largest Hispanic-owned business in the country, Burt Automotive, serve the general market in a particular metropolitan area. Still others, like the CEO of Brightstar Corporation, Marcelo Claure, have used a solid U.S. education as a springboard to starting a business that serves the regions they left. Brightstar, based in Miami but distributing cellar phones throughout Latin America, had revenues in 2003 of more than $1 billion.

The Hispanic community is strongly networked and as people start businesses or climb the career ladder, they are likely to give consideration to their countrymen for jobs. As commerce with Latin America increases, native speakers of Spanish who also speak English are increasingly desirable employees, whether in the corner convenience store or in the corporate offices of giants like Discovery Networks. In both local neighborhoods and in the international marketplace, especially since NAFTA, Hispanics have special insight into what services and products are needed and how they will be most successfully delivered.

The Marlins store described below is a good example. This is not a traditional clothing store or even a traditional team-affiliated store. Yet, it is successfully selling Marlin branded merchandise to Hispanics in Miami, in part because it is a place where Hispanics feel quite comfortable.

Hispanics have about 10 percent of U.S. buying power.

According to the Selig Center, by 2008 Hispanics will account for 9.6 percent of all U.S. buying power, up from 5.2 percent in 1990. Ten percent doesn't sound like much, but it makes a difference that it is concentrated. Of the $653 billion in Hispanic spending power in 2003, 10 states accounted for just over 80 percent. Moreover, growth in spending power is estimated to continue. The Selig Center estimates that Hispanic spending power in 2005 will be about $778 billion and that by 2008, as mentioned earlier, it will top $1 trillion.

Hispanic spending power by state, 2003 *In $U.S. billions*		Ten fastest-growing consumer markets 1990–2008 *percentage change in Hispanic buying power*	
California	$189.1	North Carolina	885.2 %
Texas	113.0	Arkansas	859.4
Florida	60.8	Georgia	660.9
New York	54.6	Tennessee	627.8
Illinois	29.7	Nevada	514.7
New Jersey	24.7	Minnesota	502.9
Arizona	19.8	Alabama	481.7
Colorado	14.2	Nebraska	442.8
New Mexico	12.9	South Carolina	427.3
Georgia	10.2	Kentucky	420.4

Source: "The Multicultural Economy 2003. America's minority buying power," The University of Georgia Selig Center.

Hispanic buying power is concentrated not only in certain states, but also in metropolitan areas within those states. Whereas nearly 19 percent of the total population lives in non-metropolitan areas, less than 9 percent of Hispanics live in those areas. Equal shares of Hispanics (about 45 percent each) live inside and outside central cities within metropolitan areas. This concentration of buying power makes it easier for retailers and their suppliers to create Hispanic strategies by carefully targeting locations and media within specific areas that have the most concentrated Hispanic buying power.

What do Hispanics spend money on?

Like most consumers, Hispanics spend on a wide range of goods and services. For many of these goods and services, their spending mirrors that of the non-Hispanic population, but in some categories Hispanics spend more than their non-Hispanic peers. These higher spending categories include groceries, telephone services, furniture, small appliances, children's clothing, and footwear. They also spend a higher proportion of their income on restaurants, housing, purchasing vehicles, and gas and motor oil.

Higher expenditures on groceries, household items, and children's clothing can be explained in part by the size of Hispanic households, which average 3.4 persons, compared with 2.4 persons in non-Hispanic households. In 2002, 30.8 percent of Mexican households had 5 or more persons. Twenty-two percent of households that contained someone of South or Central American origin had 5 or more people.

It is not surprising to see supermarkets in many parts of the country stocking more items in their Latino food departments. Not only are Hispanics big spenders on grocery items, non-Hispanic households also are making Mexican foods and other foods from South America mainstream items in their diets. The ACNielsen company's Homescan Hispanic panel details grocery purchases of Hispanic households. The panel shows, as well, how buying behavior changes as Hispanics spend more time in this country. For more on this changing buying behavior and the

Average spending per consumer unit, 2001

In U.S. dollars

	All consumers consumers	Hispanic consumers	Share of total for all consumers	Share of total for Hispanics
Food at home	$3,086	$3,551	7.8%	10.3%
Food away from home	2,235	2,097	5.7	6.1
Alcoholic beverages	349	308	0.9	0.9
Housing	13,011	11,747	32.9	34.2
Apparel & services	1,743	1,857	4.4	5.4
Transportation	7,633	7,083	19.3	20.6
Health care	2,182	1,343	5.5	3.9
Entertainment	1,953	1,246	4.9	3.6
Personal care products & services	485	467	1.2	1.4
Reading	141	59	0.4	0.2
Education	648	428	1.6	1.2
Tobacco products & smoking supplies	308	177	0.8	0.5
Miscellaneous	750	457	1.9	1.3
Cash contributions	1,258	727	3.2	2.1
Personal ins. & pensions	3,737	2,814	9.5	8.2
Total annual expenditure	39,518	34,361	100.0	100.0

Source: "The Multicultural Economy 2003. America's minority buying power," The University of Georgia Selig Center.

effects of acculturation, see *Marketing to American Latinos, Part II*, by M. Isabel Valdés. (Paramount Market Publishing, 2002).

Who are these Hispanics?

Although we speak of Hispanics in this chapter as a homogenous group, they certainly are not. Hispanics can be segmented in many different ways. They differ in their outlook and buying habits depending on their country of origin, the length of time they have spent in the United States, and their language preferences, as well as by the usual demographic segments such as age and income. Again, I refer readers to the work of M. Isabel Valdés in her excellent book, *Marketing to American Latinos: A Guide to the In-Culture Approach, Part II,* (Paramount Market Publishing, Ithaca, NY, 2002) which explains various segmentation schemes.

Briefly, of the 37.4 million Latinos in the United States in 2002 (not counting Puerto Rico), two-thirds were of Mexican origin, 14.3 percent of Central or South American origin, 8.6 percent of Puerto Rican origin, 3.7 percent of Cuban origin, and 6.5 percent of other Hispanic origins. Note the expression "of origin," used because three of five Hispanics in the United States in 2002 were born in this country, even though their parents may have been born in one of the countries mentioned above.

There are geographic differences depending on origins. Mexicans are more likely to live in the West and the South. Puerto Ricans are most likely to live in the Northeast and Cubans are most highly concentrated in the South, especially in Florida. According to the 2002 Current Population Survey, most Central and South Americans were found in three of the four regions, the Northeast, the South, and the West. The Midwest has fewer Hispanics, but that is changing rapidly.

By age, Cubans are the oldest Hispanic group, with 22.6 percent of them aged 65 and older. Mexicans are the youngest, with 37.1 percent of them under age 18. Overall, the Hispanic population is younger than the non-Hispanic white population in the United States. This age disparity means that a large share of the entry-level labor force in this country will be Hispanic and that Hispanic culture will likely continue to become mainstream as the younger generations set the cultural trends in our country.

Because we can predict that Hispanics will be an important part of the entry-level labor force in the future, it is important to note that more than two in five Hispanics aged 25 and over have not graduated from high school. One-quarter of Hispanics aged 25 and older in 2002 had less than a ninth grade education, compared with only 4 percent of non-Hispanic whites. Mexicans are the least likely to have graduated from high school.

Employers have to be aware of the deficiencies in the education of some Hispanics and be prepared to invest in training for their employees. The lack of education among Hispanics is also an opportunity for employers who can offer GED classes or scholarship programs for teenage employees. In many areas, there may be increased opportunities for adult education and organizations that offer adult education are usually delighted to meet the needs of the business community in their choice of subjects.

Population with at least a high school education by Hispanic origin
Percent of each population aged 25 and older

Non-Hispanic White	88.7%
Mexican	50.6
Puerto Rican	66.8
Cuban	70.8
Central & South American	64.7
Other Hispanic	74.0

Source: The Hispanic Population in the United States: March 2002, Current Population Reports, P20-545, U.S. Census Bureau.

Hispanic workers were hard hit by the recession in late 1999 to 2003. At the time of the 2002 Current Population Survey, only 26 percent of Hispanics overall were employed in full-time, year-round work with annual earnings of $35,000 or more. Mexicans and Puerto Ricans were most likely to be living below the poverty line.

continues page 10 . . .

Lessons from the Street

The Siesta Concept:
Marlins en Miami

During the 2003 National League Divisional playoffs between the Florida Marlins and the Chicago Cubs, my wife and I were in Miami cheering for our team from Chicago. I hadn't been able to find a souvenir hat I wanted at Pro Player Stadium, home of the Marlins. When I came across Marlins en Miami, a retail store located at the very west end of colorful Calle Ocho, I went in.

Being bilingual I did not realize that Marlins en Miami was not Marlins in Miami. The simple use of "en" versus "in" was geared toward the Cuban, Spanish-preferred fan, not the English-preferred fan.

As I entered the store, there sat a Miami police officer, frequently lifting his head and acknowledging incoming customers. The sales associate, with no name tag, greeted us with, "Hola" and continued on with her responsibilities. The store itself was not the best example of how to manage, nor present a product, especially a seasonal product. At that time of the year seasonal sales surrounding baseball would usually be well past their peak. However the Marlins were battling the Cubs for the National League Championship.

Few of the items had a price tag as I looked for the hat I wanted among jerseys, shirts, ball bats, and baseball novelty items. Most retailers know that a customer will not ask the price, merely move along and not purchase!

It was at this point the journey started. My wife had made it known we were Cubs fans. Only the sales associate and the lady behind us in the checkout line of six people acknowledged us. We thought that was odd, assuming that Cubs fans in Miami would provoke conversation.

Then, the lady behind us, in a perfectly fashioned Cuban-American accent—the kind one earns only after years in Miami and time away from Calle Ocho —said, "I am interested to know why are you shopping here? This is Marlins en Miami, the Spanish-speaking store, mostly frequented by Cuban Americans!"

I did not feel ill at ease at her question, but it was at this point that my wife who is South Korean and I, with my blue eyes and English and Polish ancestry became the oddities. Perhaps we both felt how Spanish-preferred Latinos feel when they are in an English-dominant restaurant or grocery store in other parts of our country.

The Cuban lady continued to tell me that Cubans love baseball and that this store is closer than the store located on the other side of Miami. She said Cubans feel more comfortable shopping at this store because it is a store where they can communicate. Not only is it close, it is also "in-language" for the customer.

For some Cubans, she told me, this store is their only contact with the Marlins. "Many of us don't drive and don't feel comfortable on public transportation. This is the store for us."

As I continued to listen, I realized that the shopping process inside of Marlins en Miami was relaxed, comfortable, and inviting, even though the product was not priced and the selection was not terrific. The constant buzz from customer to sales associate of *"Cuanto Vale?"* (How Much?) was part of the process that allowed all of us to say, *"Bastante."* (Too Much.), yet walk up to the register with the item in our hand.

The checkout line was long—at least six people. Most associates in retail are taught to scan the merchandise, bag it, count back change, and move the customer through the line.

Not here! This Marlins en Miami built into its store the passion for the game and the passion of its fans in this neighborhood. Ultimately the goal was conversation. The entire process was built around dialogue, around baseball, around an exchange. In exchange for the product, the sales associate received cash but the customer received the overwhelming experience of baseball "in language." This is a fundamental of marketing, a positive exchange must occur!

No, the transaction was not as quick as purchasing food at fast-food chains. The product was not priced and properly displayed by Anglo standards. But it was a safe haven for the Cuban-speaking fan. It was in a sense a domino game being played with a friend underneath swaying palm trees that block the intense Florida sun. Does a Cuban play dominos for the game or for the conversation?

Marlins en Miami is conversational. It is a coffee lounge without the coffee where baseball and sport are part of the retail experience.

As we left the store my wife asked the police officer, "Why are *you* here?" His reply, "Last week it was so busy, $15,000 per day busy, that Miami news anchors arrived and traffic needed to be controlled."

Fifteen Thousand! Not bad for a 1,000 square foot, not-so-well merchandised store.

However, given the Hispanic buying power reported above, the data on poverty have to be reviewed by city and neighborhood. Overall, Hispanic married-couple households in 2002 had a median annual income of $40,614. Female householders with children but no male present had the lowest median annual income at $20,547, consistent with the pattern shown across racial and ethnic lines.

It is well understood that workers are at their peak earning years in their forties and fifties. Given that the median age of Hispanics in the work force is 26.3 years compared with 37.3 years for non-Hispanics, it is not surprising that their incomes are lower than those of non-Hispanic households and it makes sense that their incomes will rise as they age and have more job experience.

There is a good case for creating Hispanic marketing strategies now within all kinds of companies that supply goods and services. The lessons learned in the most concentrated markets mentioned above will help retailers especially to make good site and positioning decisions in the future as Hispanics disseminate even further into the heartland.

Lesson learned . . .

Big and small retailers alike often follow a concept, building their stores the way they have always been built and stocking them with the same merchandise from store to store. I do not suggest this is wrong. However, in Latin neighborhoods, there is an opportunity for ingenuity and creativity. Customer dwell time also must be taken into consideration. Call it the "siesta concept." Call it *conversación*, call it what you will but in addition to language, it is an important lesson in the Latino purchasing process that drives repeat business.

Lessons from the Street

A note on Customer Dwell Time

At malls across the U.S., benches and comfortable chairs are strategically placed so as to increase dwell time or time spent inside of the mall. The same is true for many business' south of the boarder. Take for example the Oxxo Convenience Stores in Mexico. The largest convenience store group in Mexico is certainly interested in moving the maximum number of customers through their doors on a daily basis, but they have also built into their store design two small tables near the doorway for their customers to enjoy their lunch or snack. While a convenience store chain operating in the U.S. may not consider this, in Mexico it is commonplace based on the customer wanting a place to relax and eat. And who knows, maybe this customer purchases additional items based on being in the store longer.

Thus, remember sales can be driven and increased by and through language and also by incorporating culture into the dialogue of the store.

The following chapters will describe specific points and programs that should be considered for a successful Hispanic strategy that goes *Beyond Bodegas*.

CHAPTER 2

Why Length of Time in Country Matters

Prior to the 1970s few major retailers sold their goods to ethnic markets. This was usually left to the small immigrant manufacturers and retailers in corner "mom and pop" stores who advertised in church bulletins or through the pages of foreign language press. Today however, American corporations are spending millions to ensure ethnic consumers are stocking their cupboards and refrigerators with branded products.

It took Madison Avenue little time to realize that the buying habits of Poles, Jews, Irish, Greeks, Italians, Chinese, Cubans and other ethnic groups were connected closely and idiosyncratic. Thus, these groups could be segmented. Marketers studied and surveyed and re-surveyed ethnic populations and broke them down into groups and subgroups, including by the amount of time they had spent in this country. They began to perfect the methodologies used to reach the groups and the subgroups. New segmentations were developed based on shopping trip practices and activities as well as attitudes and lifestyle measures.

In a 2002 report called, *U.S. Hispanics: Insights into Grocery Shopping Preferences and Attitude,* the Food Marketing Institute identified four groups of grocery shoppers among Hispanics. They are Economists, Loyalists, Pricehunters, and Traditionalists. The following table shows distinguishing features of the four groups.

The four groups of grocery shoppers among Hispanics

Economists	Loyalists	Pricehunters	Traditionalists
Bilingual	Spanish Preferred	Spanish Preferred	Spanish Dominant
One-third born in U.S. Rest have lived in U.S. an average of 18 years	15 percent born in the U.S.	13 percent born in U.S.; 62 percent born in Mexico	9 percent born in U.S., 65 percent born in Mexico
Average Age: 42	Average Age: 39	Average Age: 39	Average Age: 40
Less likely to have children at home	Young family households	Households with children	Households with children
Average household income: $29,800	Average household income: $22,420	Average household income: $23,380	Average household income: $20,880
More likely to shop alone	Are loyal to their primary store	Shop at multiple stores for best prices	Shop at multiple stores for traditional Hispanic products
Stock-up on sale items	Not influenced by advertising or promotions	Will try new brands if on sale	The least satisfied with their primary store
Heavily influenced by sale items	Risk aversive	Very price sensitive	Brand loyal and risk aversive
Do not set a budget for grocery shopping	Prepare shopping lists and stick to them	Engage in price comparisons	Set budget for grocery shopping
Hispanic elements not important	Hispanic elements are important	Hispanic elements are important	Hispanic elements are very important
Spend $111 per week on groceries	Spend $112 per week on groceries	Spend $111 per week on groceries	Spend $121 per week on groceries

Source: *U.S. Hispanics: Insights into Grocery Shopping Preferences and Attitudes, 2002.*
© 2002, Food Marketing Institute, Washington, DC. (www.fmi.org) Used by permission.

One important element in distinguishing various groups of Hispanic shoppers is the length of time that the shopper has lived in this country. Numerous studies have found that shopping behavior changes as immigrants move from being new arrivals to being more acculturated. The less acculturated are closely related to the Traditionalists in the chart above.

An example of how to appeal to foreign-born consumers can be found in The Mega Mall on Milwaukee Avenue on Chicago's Northwest side. This mall is a cinder block building painted various colors. It has a tin roof, few windows, no advertising, is the size of a football field, and has a parking lot for about ten cars on one side. The preferred language once inside is not English.

On a cold January day I visited the Mega Mall and was struck with what I considered to be the chaos and replication of products from vendor to vendor. The inside is a cornucopia of merchandise—a junkyard of stuff sold from at least 50 vendors. Independent retailers sell gold, Mexican silver, cowboy hats and boots, Mexican soccer jerseys and imported candies, underwear, socks, sports shoes, urban-youth wear, tools, stereo equipment, athletic shoes, CDs, Elvis pictures, and my favorite, specialized window tenting for warm Chicago days.

The atmosphere itself is similar to a swap meet, but this Mega Mall is open daily. No merchandising, no pricing, no controls, items are hung, stacked, stuck, shoved, and layered. The building itself is poorly lit, the kiosks of merchandise are separated by rope and an odd deep-fried smell permeates the entire place.

I talked with a young Mexican girl in charge of the family kiosk, a candy outlet. Brands like Carlos V., Duvalín, Lucas, and de la Rosa were displayed at knee height. Hanging from the walls were sour worms, sweet and sour suckers, tamarindo, and hot peanuts. I bought a tamarindo sweet, opened it and asked this young Mexican girl, "Who shops here and why?"

She responded, "People who have just arrived and want a taste from the home land—a brand from the home land. They shop here because it is cheap and they can walk. They also shop here because it reminds them of the markets in Mexico; they can touch it and feel it."

"Have you been to a market in Mexico?" I asked. She replied, "I am 19 and visiting from Mexico. This is a family owned business and we all live in Mexico and take turns running this place. These are items you just can't find in a 7-Eleven."

While I don't suggest you throw away your plan-o-grams, note the following from the above example:

- Being able to segment your shoppers into the four groups described in the table above will help you create an environment and merchandise a store which is compatible with your specific consumer. Don't assume your customer base will be composed of all four.

- Understanding the local acculturation at your place of business will allow you to build an effective marketing and advertising campaign. As in the case of the Mega Mall, no plan may be visible, but a plan does exist.

Language preference is dynamic and changes with acculturation

In its study of U.S. Hispanic shoppers, the Food Marketing Institute also looked at language preference. Most studies segment Hispanics into the following language categories: English-Preferred, Spanish-Preferred, and Bilinguals. Normally, the degree of English or Spanish proficiency is linked to the level of acculturation—the more Spanish Hispanic consumers prefer, the less acculturated they are. The more English Hispanic consumers prefer, the more acculturated they are likely to be.

U.S. Hispanic language preference

	Spanish-Preferred	Bilingual	English-Preferred
Percentage in sample	65%	30%	5%
Country of Origin			
Born in U.S.	3%	40%	78%
Foreign Born	97	60	22
Average number of years in the U.S.	13	20	31
Education			
Some High School or Less	62%	38%	27%
College Graduate or More	10	38	37
Household Income Levels			
Under $15,000	47%	21%	22%
$15,000 – $34,999	35	31	16
$35,000 or More	5	35	47

Source: *U.S. Hispanics: Insights into Grocery Shopping Preferences and Attitudes, 2002.*
© 2002, Food Marketing Institute, Washington, DC. (www.fmi.org). Used by permission.

The Food Marketing Institute report explains:

"English-Preferred Hispanics are predominantly born in the United States and have lived in this country an average of 31 years. The consumer preferences of this U.S. Hispanic group will be similar to those of the general U.S. marketplace. Approximately 40 percent of Bilingual Hispanics were born in the United States and they have lived here for an average of 20 years. English-Preferred Hispanics and Bilinguals have higher education and income levels than Spanish-Preferred Hispanics.

"In contrast, over 97 percent of Spanish-Preferred Hispanics are foreign born, with 70 percent born in Mexico. Their average length of residence in the United States is 13 years. Unlike English-Preferred households, Spanish-Preferred households are far more likely to have children in the home.

"Although acculturation is an inevitable process, U.S. Hipanics maintain a strong desire to be connected to their roots. Nearly eight out of 10 U.S. Hispanics indicate they want to stay connected to their countries of origin. Moreover, while 86 percent of U.S. Hispanics strongly agree that they want their children to speak English well, 85 percent also strongly agree that it is important for their children to speak Spanish just as well."

Less acculturated

According to *DNS Retailing Today*,[1] less acculturated Hispanics "tend to shop fewer alternative outlets, such as warehouse clubs and mass merchants, and buy products they've grown up with in their country of origin."

As U.S. Hispanics become comfortable with the U.S. way of life, they are more likely to venture out and away from their own neighborhoods. With time, there is not only a whole new world but also a whole new retail space for the consumer. As acculturation increases, retailers who once attracted Hispanic consumers simply because they were in the right neighborhood may be challenged to establish store loyalty and marketing programs to keep these customers.

The Food Marketing Institute study cited above found that the number of store visits per month increases for the more acculturated—the Economists and Loyalists—and that the range of type of food retailer visited also increases with acculturation.

---

1 "Los Angeles Latinos Ring the Cash Registers" Special Report on Ethnic Marketing , July 21, 2003. www.dnsretailingtoday.com

As noted in an earlier discussion about the Mexican girl at the candy store, transportation is also an issue. In large cities, less acculturated Hispanic households are less likely to have cars or they may share a car with other households. Therefore, they tend to shop at stores within walking distance of their homes, or to carpool to supercenters and discount warehouses. Because they are limited by transportation, the number of different types of retailers that they visit may be limited. ACNielsen reports that Hispanics that prefer or speak only English are more likely to shop at mass market outlets and club channels than those who prefer or speak only Spanish.

Retail environments based on consumer's time in the country

A generation of American Hispanics has been in this country a long time and expects retailers to recognize their dual cultures. Hispanics today are often treated as a niche audience but their numbers alone should gain marketer's full attention. Hispanics are the largest and fastest-growing ethnic group in America. In addition, today 20 percent of U.S. births are to Hispanic mothers. With 70 percent of the nation's 37 million Hispanics under the age of 30, they represent a captive audience for retailers and business of all shapes and sizes.

For this younger generation, it's no longer about assimilating into American culture. Assimilation is old and cumbersome terminology and has yielded to the new, more refreshing term: acculturation, or retaining one's native culture while incorporating it into what it suggests to be American. It's about being Mexican *and* American, Cuban *and* American, Puerto Rican *and* American. Today's young Hispanics have two lives: They listen to hip hop with friends and dance to salsa at home, watch *novelas* in Spanish with the parents but instant message with their classmates on the computer.

With feedback from Hispanic shoppers, retailers are learning about different food preferences and how much product to offer without alienating mainstream customers. Ethnic supermarkets such as Fiesta, and Carnival in Texas, specialize in meeting the Hispanic shopper's needs, while super-center operators such as Wal-Mart have expanded the assortment of Hispanic food and integrated it into existing displays depending on neighborhood demand.

Retail elements

A closer look at the retail environment suggests that specifically tailored environments composed of Hispanic elements play an important role for Latinos when they are deciding where to shop. When Hispanic grocery shoppers were asked the importance of various language elements and product offerings in the retail environment, Hispanic elements rated high for at least two-thirds of those surveyed, as shown in the table below.

Hispanic elements rated as very important in deciding
where to shop for food products

Percent of those surveyed who said this element was very important

Bilingual employees	79%
Employees knowledgeable about Hispanic products	78
Sells Hispanic products	76
Bilingual store signs	70
Bilingual packaging on food items	68
Carries imported Hispanic food Items	68

Source: *U.S. Hispanics: Insights into Grocery Shopping Preferences and Attitudes, 2002.*
© 2002, Food Marketing Institute, Washington, DC. (www.fmi.org)

Digging deeper into this, U.S. Hispanics not only prefer to

shop at stores where they are able to speak Spanish, but they also want to purchase products associated with their tastes. For the less acculturated, the environment needs to feel relaxed and comfortable. As the study cited above indicates, bilingual circulars and signs, Spanish-speaking employees, and carrying products familiar to these customers should help. Retailers may provide transportation or offer *Servicio a Domicilio* (home delivery) for those who don't drive. Retailers who offer fresh meat products may want to hire a butcher who is familiar with such cuts of meat at bistec and jalisco pork, a simple version of *carne adobado,* pork marinated in a sauce of chile, garlic, and vinegar with cumin and oregano preferred by Hispanic shoppers.

DNS Retailing Today reports, that one reason it is worth providing this extra service is that "the amount spent on UPC-coded items per average grocery trip by a Hispanic shopper is $37. That is $10 more than $27 spent by the Anglo shopper. That number may be even higher considering many Hispanics cook from scratch and buy more non-UPC coded fresh produce, meat, and seafood than the typical American household. . . . Fruit drinks, tomato sauce, and carbonated soft drinks are also high on this shopper's list, according to AC Nielsen, while canned soup and diet drinks are of less interest."

U.S. Hispanics: Insights into Grocery Shopping Preferences and Attitudes 2002 reports that Latino households spend 17 percent to 50 percent more on meat, produce, dairy, and cereal than the typical shopper.

Brand offering at home vs. U.S.

For many Hispanics their first experience with a U.S. brand is in their home country. If they liked a brand or store they found in their home country, they are likely to continue to prefer it when they come to the United States. There was no question in my mind as an employee of Grupo Chapa's 7-Eleven, Mexico team that the stores we had were better designed and merchandised, and cleaner because of the involvement we had from our friends in the U.S. Thus, 7-Eleven in the U.S. may be preferred in certain markets and for these Mexican immigrants, the preference and experience started in Mexico. Hispanics cross the border as brand loyalists to certain brands and many of their products. A brand like Coca-Cola is so entrenched, that consumers may be reluctant to try something else. However, as the consumer becomes more acculturated or more willing to try different brands, the competitive advantage may begin to diminish.

M. Isabel Valdés in her book, *Marketing to American Latinos, A Guide to the In-Culture Approach, Part 2* explains: "Global brands that are heavily marketed in countries outside the United States often enjoy 'brand heritage' and get a lift when foreigners move to the U.S. These companies could lose this competitive advantage when they choose to market the same product under different brand names in the U.S. or foreign countries."

As reported in *The Wall Street Journal Online*[2], Guatemala's Pollo Campero, SA is an example from the Quick Serve Restaurant sector. It opened its first U.S. restaurant in 2003. Chains from Brazil, Mexico, and Venezuela offer everything from pork tacos to fried sugared dough, or *churros*. Again, these restaurants want to trade on their brand recognition with Hispanic immigrants. If they are lucky, they can also capture the mainstream U.S. consumer who is open to trying new foods.

Harry Balzer, vice president of NPD Group, a consumer-marketing research firm in Port Washington, N.Y. is quoted in the WSJ.com article as saying, "We are seeing development of new fast-food concepts like we haven't seen in maybe 20 years,"

---

2 Bouza, Teresa and Gabriel Sama, "New Franchise Outlets Serve Changing Tastes" date www.wsjonline.com

and each of the chains is entering the U.S. primarily to cater to Latino immigrants and Hispanic-Americans—filling an under-served market.

Taking lessons from Mexicans

Attendees at the 2004 Expo ANTAD in Guadalajara, Mexico in March 2004, saw many recognizable U.S. brands. ANTAD (Aso-ciación Nacional de Tiendas de Autoservicio y Departamentales) or the National Association of Self-service and Department Stores was established in 1983 to represent the legitimate inter-ests of its associates and promote the development of retail com-merce and its suppliers in order to satisfy the consumers' needs.

At the ANTAD Expo, suppliers from Mexico as well as com-panies from the U.S. and other countries set their sights on the Mexican marketplace by displaying food, beverages, tech-nology, and support to the food industry. Procter & Gamble and Colgate led the way with two of the larger and best-presented displays at the entire event, which consisted of more than 1,000 food vendors and suppliers.

5 al Día: Mexico's current national fruit campaign

During a presentation at ANTAD Nancy Tucker, vice president of Global Development for the Produce Marketing Association noted, "In the United States, the majority of fruit and vegetables are consumed by people aged 50 and older and married. Young families with children under age 12 and mothers under age 35 consume the least amount of fruit. In contrast, in Mexico fruit is essential to the health of children and promoted as needed for a good balanced diet."

Principal reasons that limit the purchase of fruit in the U.S.

Percent of people who gave this reason

Reason	Percent
Poor quality	56%
Too expensive	50
Not available	34
Poor merchandising	14
Seasonal	6

Source: The Packer Fresh Trends, 2003, Vance Publications, Volume 54. Survey was conducted by mail and email of a random sample of 1,136 households between July 8 and August 5, 2002. Special thanks to Nate Gulliford at Vance Publications.

Thus, with Mexican-Americans composing the majority of U.S. Hispanics, it would be wise for the U.S. food retailer to cater to this consumer's needs and habits. The Food Marketing Institute report also noted that 97 percent of all U.S. Hispanics rank fresh, high-quality fruits and vegetables as very important in deciding where to shop.

In July 2004 I had the opportunity to chat with Nancy Tucker following her return from a business trip to South Africa. She suggested that U.S. retailers must understand the need to build displays of fruit and vegetables that allow the U.S. Hispanic to feel comfortable with the display and the interaction with the fruit on the displays. Design, lighting, service, produce selection and availability are all contributing factors of interaction and in order to understand this, retailers must understand the buying habits in the native land of many of their customers.

Switching continents, Ms. Tucker continued with a colorful story about a major retailer in Hong Kong who wants to take indoors what is currently outdoors on the streets of Hong Kong—produce. On the street in Hong Kong, people know that the produce is fresh daily and the employees help customers bag and weigh their purchases. It is the same with the outdoor markets in Latin America and for a retailer to be successful, the same type of atmosphere needs to be created here in the U.S.. I asked Ms. Tucker if the Hong Kong street market is similar in style and atmosphere to the produce and fish market of China Town in San Francisco and she said, "Yes, same idea, same freshness and same interactive atmosphere, same perceived chaos."

Some final thoughts

- If a major player like Coca-Cola is investing in the Hispanic segment, you should do more than just consider it. Too often I hear, "I am not convinced." Montgomery Wards was not convinced of its need to change retailing practices and it is now extinct. Don't allow this to be your future.

- The more acculturated the more comfortable. The less acculturated the less comfortable. I have certainly seen areas where the two segments live side by side, but the more acculturated tend to spread their wings and try new neighborhoods, products, and schools. What you think you know versus what you actually know is critical. The foundation for success is research.

- Develop credibility for your retail outlet by recognizing and providing food products relevant to the Hispanic's taste and traditions.

- Understanding the segment will allow you to target. Whether your customer is English-preferred, Spanish-preferred, Bilingual, or from the Caribbean, South America or Mexico, it is worth reiterating, that not all Hispanics possess the same taste preferences and food profiles.

- As a retailer, do more to attract and keep Hispanic shoppers. As a suggestion, introduce them to frequent shopper programs. Offer in-language sign-up materials and inform them how the information will be used and that it will not be shared. This will assist in keeping less-acculturated consumers, once they begin to spread their wings.

- Stay loyal to your business model. If you are a retailer catering to the general public, but with Hispanics as a percentage of your customer base, incorporate Hispanic items, language, and crossover music. Your business is to remember what you do best, yet recognize an opportunity while understanding how the decisions you make impact your existing customer base.

- Stay attuned to the brand preferences of Hispanic shoppers. Carry the products, make sure you don't run out, and do your best to earn this group's loyalty. Those that do will be positioned to benefit from future population shifts as Hispanics grow in number.

CHAPTER 3

Marketing In-Culture

Retailers in search of better understanding of how growth in the Hispanic consumer market is affecting many communities, need only drive through their community, attend a town hall meeting, look at who is attending school, playing Little League, and who is opening Hispanic-themed grocery stores

As explained in chapter one, clusters of Hispanics exist in most urban areas, with the southwest and the western states being the most concentrated. However, many small towns all across America are experiencing growth in Hispanic's presence and spending power.

The retailer must understand how the ethnic background of a given population affects its consumption habits and purchasing behavior, as U.S. Hispanic consumers continue to demonstrate their distinct tastes to both the retailer and manufacturer.

A look at the global music industry may be helpful and when studying how to modify local strategies in order to earn the respect of U.S. Hispanic consumers and take advantage of opportunities they represent. Music, like athletic sports, courtship, ethics, language, and marriage is universally accepted as a form of expression. It is also a source of entertainment. Music serves as a real-life example of capturing culture and the tastes associated with different cultures.

Music is part of culture, characterized by varying styles. Thus, the type of music that can be used effectively in commercials or at the local retail level as background music may need to vary because Hispanic consumers, like the general population, have a variety of tastes in music. These tastes can also vary by region and country of origin. For example, a jingle in a supermarket in Miami may use a Cuban *chachachá*, whereas in San Antonio, Texas *Norteña* may be a better choice because it is closely related to the Mexican community there. You should also be aware that new artists, and new sounds are constantly coming of age in the global market. At the local level, you can identify new sounds, new acts, and new artists, and then use these new talents and sounds to help demonstrate your understanding of the market.

Here's another example, outside of the music industry. The Mexican bread company, Bimbo, long a favorite in its domestic market, has been keenly aware of the potential of extending its successful bread making business across the border to the United States. It has bread making down. Certainly operational differences may exist from plant to plant, but product and quality remain consistent. Today its tasty line of Bimbo bread products can be found at many stores selling to U.S. Hispanics.

If you understand value creation, whether you sell cars, pharmaceuticals, convenience products or manage department stores or internet companies, you can adapt your business for customers with varying cultural backgrounds. Though the content of your

Hispanic Population in Top Ten U.S. Hispanic Markets *population in millions*	
Orange County, Riverside, Los Angeles, CA	6.75
New York, New Jersey, Long Island, NY	4.1
Miami–Ft. Lauderdale	1.7
Chicago, IL, East Chicago, IN, Racine and Kenosa, WI	1.7
San Francisco, Oakland and San Jose, CA	1.4
Houston–Port Arthur– Galveston	1.35
Dallas–Ft. Worth, TX	1.1
San Antonio, TX	.9
San Diego, CA	.753
San Juan, Arecibo and Caguas	2.4
Source: U.S. Census 2000	

product or good remains basically the same from market to market, the process of creating value for your Hispanic customers will vary. Stay in tune with the market place and refrain from applying generic principals to a heterogeneous market.

At your bank or car dealership, it should not matter to you if the entire family shows up to open a bank account or comes to buy a car dressed in fancy attire. What you may consider normal is based on your experience with the world in which you live. The behavior may be different than what you would expect, but the money is green! To be successful you must understand the human experience from the point of view of your customers. When the customers experience is understood, the dynamics or pulse of your shop will likely be an amalgam of numerous ethnicities and nations, while still allowing you to do whatever it is you do best.

On the way home from a meeting I stopped at LA Motors in downtown Los Angeles. It was Sunday night and the car dealership was open for business. There were bilingual advertisements, and the smell of freshly grilled quesadillas filled the air. Soft salsa and *ranchera* music played in the background. I spoke to a young salesman, Lance Hong. Lance told me that the Mexican-American customers enjoy the lively atmosphere and the bilingual sales approach, as well as the bilingual credit counseling the dealership has. He said, "It is the way we do business for our Hispanic customers. We also know they come into the store with a car in mind, and we do very little to suggest a different model or add-ons. It does not sit well with them."

Here's another example: An independent grocer in Indiana modified his store to include a Mexican category in both the meat department and vegetable area. At the time he was concerned that some of the Polish-American customers who had traded with him for 15 years might not understand the change. He wanted to please all his customers, yet he had to be prepared to explain why some Polish products were discontinued—a move that might be interpreted as being pushed out of the store due to the introduction of Mexican goods. He told his Polish-American customers, "I have been a neighborhood grocer for many years and my job is to serve our community. Our community is now mixed and I care about my customers. If I can hold retail prices down by introducing new products and removing slower moving ones, it will be good for all of us."

He told me he had to use that answer only once. What he hadn't realized, he said, was that the neighborhood around him was changing and accepting, while he was inside his little world filled with preoccupations and, at times, prejudice. As I ended the conversation with this grocer, a young boy came up and said, "Hi, my name is Carlos Lupinski. I speak Spanish, English, and Polish and just heard your conversation. Thanks. Where else can I buy fresh salsa, Polish Chocolate, Red Bull, and Captain Crunch—all in the same place?"

High Context, Low Context Cultures

Anthropologist Edward T. Hall in *Beyond Culture* (Garden City, NY, Anchor Press Doubleday, 1976) outlined the concept of high and low context culture as a means of understanding cultural differences. In a high-context culture, much more information is contained in the communication process, including the background, associations and basic values of the parties or communicators involved. High-context cultures function with much less formality. A low-context culture, in contrast, relies on the written word. Messages are explicit and written words convey the majority of information in communication.

My interview process with 7-Eleven of Mexico was more about relationships and conversation than filling out paper work. It was more about how I fit into the organization and how I could serve it, rather than whether I could read a pro forma financial statement or investigate future real estate opportunities. The interview was filled with relationship building and bonding, definitely an example of a high-context cultural interaction.

In a high-context culture, the relationship is the bond. The culture emphasizes trust and shared obligations and honor. These values replace impersonal memos and legal sanctions. This understanding should help retailers, churches, bankers, and others understand why some customers are slow to respond to a place of business or a proposed deal. In a high-context culture, extended and prolonged courtship exists and lunch and golf come prior to the deal as a means to communicate. It takes time to build trust.

In street terms, high context is about the retailer who may be willing to extend credit to a customer because cash is gone and payday is tomorrow, but the kids need to eat and the car needs gas.

Shaking your head? It happens! My friend Kris, owns a Mobil gas station in Van Nuys, California on Burbank Boulevard. Many of his customers owe him cash for gas or a gallon of milk and a pack of cigarettes. Kris explains, "This is my community. Where I come from—Iraq—we took care of each other. My customers are the parents of children, just like me. Their kids and my kids go to the same school. For the most part, I limit it but I am paid. Just because these folks don't carry a credit card does not mean I don't do business with them!"

Really shaking your head? Imagine this. Charles A. Coombs was a Senior VP of the Federal Reserve Bank in New York, in charge of foreign exchange operations. The world of the central banker as he describes it is a 'gentlemen's world' that has a high-context culture. In his book, *The Arena of International Finance* (John Wiley & Sons, September 1976) he writes about how the central banker's word is sufficient for him to borrow millions of dollars. During rioting and political upheavals in France in the mid-1970s, central bankers' confidence in one another was dramatically demonstrated. With the exception of phones, communications between France and the U.S. were not functioning. Consequently, the New York Fed agreed to follow telephone instructions from the Bank of France to intervene on its behalf in support of the then French franc. Within eight days, the New York Fed purchased more than $50 million worth of francs without a single written confirmation for any part of the purchase. Yes, the Fed was out on a limb, but Coombs understood how to work with France.

Two weeks later the daughter of a governor of the Bank of France came to New York on personal business. With her she brought all the written confirmations. Coombs breathed a sigh of relief. He was acting in high-context culture in which his word is his bond, but his legal department was living in a low-context culture. They needed it in writing and all should have been agreed upon among the parties involved prior to the transaction.

Elements of High and Low Context

Factors/Dimensions	High Context	Low Context
Bankers	Less Important	Extremely Important
Lawyers	Less Important	Very Important
Priests/Clergy	Very Important	Less Important
Space	People breath on each other	Barriers exist, intrusion is resented
Negotiations	Lengthy, I need to know this person. Conversation.	Now, Yesterday
Time	Polychronic: Everything in life will be dealt with in time	Monochronic: Time is cash. Linear: one item at a time
Country Examples	Japan, Middle East, some Latin American Countries	United States, Canada, Northern Europe

Source: Keegan, Warren J., *Global Marketing Management*, 7th Edition, © 2002. Reprinted by permission of Pearson Education, Inc., Upper Saddle River, NJ.

For corporate America and the car dealers, franchisees, bottlers, banks, and manufacturers, and the brands they represent, in order to advance in doing business with the Hispanic cultures, a certain amount of formality must be relinquished.

Misperceptions

Many manufacturers and retailers are still suffering under the misperception that all Hispanics are immigrants, poor, and under-educated. A 2001 study completed by the Tomas Rivera Policy Institute found that Hispanics are quickly joining the ranks of the middle class. Thirty-five percent of all Hispanic households had reached the middle class—defined as those having an annual income exceeding $40,000 in 1998—whereas 42 percent of U.S.-born Hispanics had reached the middle class.

There are differences among recent immigrants and those who are U.S. born, but they are narrowing.

Income: Income levels will vary by time in country. Those who have recently arrived suggest the experience for the new Hispanic arrival to be similar to that of other immigrant groups. As is seen in the table below, as language skills increase or language preference moves towards bilingual and English preferred among Latinos, so does household income.

Language skills and household income levels

	Spanish-preferred	Bilingual	English-preferred
Percentage in sample	65%	30%	5%
Household Income			
Under $15,000	47%	21%	22%
$15,000-$34,999	35%	31%	16%
$35,000 or more	5 %	35%	47%

Source: U.S. Hispanics: Insights into Grocery Shopping Preferences and Attitudes,2002. © 2002, Food Marketing Institute, Washington, DC. (www.fmi.org)

Education: Native-born Hispanics and the college educated are catching up. According to the Hispanic Fact Sheet published in January 2002 by the Pew Hispanic Center, "The growing earnings gap between Hispanics and whites partly reflects the fact that recent Latino immigrants comprise 40 percent of all Hispanics. Over time immigrant wages improve, but lower average education holds down their earnings potential. In fact, studies show that all, or nearly all, of the wage gap between white and Hispanic workers can be explained by gaps in English skills and education. For Hispanic and non-Hispanic white workers with similar skills, there is virtually no wage gap."

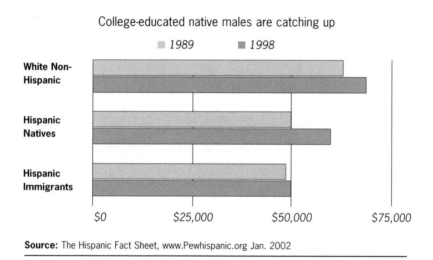

College-educated native males are catching up

■ 1989   ■ 1998

Source: The Hispanic Fact Sheet, www.Pewhispanic.org Jan. 2002

A national survey of Latinos by the Pew Hispanic Center in January 2004 found that nearly 95 percent of Latinos felt that young people starting out today have little chance of success without a college degree. Knowing this, it is not surprising that nearly all Latino parents say it is very important to them that their children go to college.

Retailers and communities alike must realize that Latinos are becoming more educated and more informed over time. As more and more young Latinos have the opportunity to finish high school and college, this trend will accelerate. The U.S. Census Bureau reports that people aged 5 to 24 make up 37 percent of the Hispanic population compared with 27 percent of the non-Hispanic population. Moreover, during the next 25 years, this segment of the Latino population is projected to increase by 82 percent, according to projections by the Pew Hispanic Center. What buying power is in their future!

Culture Modifiers

Cultural modifiers are those attributes, which distinguish one culture from another. It may be as simple as tea drinking versus coffee drinking. For example, Americans prefer a sweet ketchup, but most Europeans prefer a spicier more piquant variety. Heinz therefore adapts to the local cultural preferences. In Sweden, Heinz's usual foreign marketing efforts supporting made in America is de-emphasized and many Swedes don't realize Heinz is American.

In another example, one of my friends from Mexico City, Adrianna, recently told me that her family's refrigerator at home in Mexico City has a freezer section that is never used because food is always purchased fresh. What an insight about differences in food purchasing and the lack of frozen food purchased by Mexicans.

Basically, learning about another culture and seeing how a product or service fits into it is a two-way street.

- When a culture or buying habit is studied, we increase our sensitivity to and knowledge of cultures other than our own and thus we build our understanding of the culture.

- At the same time, the people being asked the questions or being studied feel valued because their diversity and background is brought to the forefront and they are able to show their pride.

Martha De La Vega is the Associate Director of La Villita Chamber of Commerce in Chicago. Martha opened the doors of La Villita and allowed me the opportunity to learn more about this booming, predominantly Mexican area of Chicago.

Martha was raised in Pilsen, Chicago's rich and proud Mexican village. Martha is a Chicana and a graduate of Northern Illinois University and shows pride for her community. She is outgoing, energetic, and speaks about La Villita as if she had worked in the community for 30 years; in reality Martha can't be a day older than 25. She is bilingual and her parents are from Mexico and prefer Spanish inside the home.

I admire Martha's sensitivity to the community. When speaking of the chamber members she describes two different types of members. "The group under age 45 is bilingual and normally have benefited from their parents. When we solicit them to become members, they ask us for our website or to please send us the information and benefits associated with membership in the mail."

"Our over-age 45 business owners, who are the pioneers to this area, journeyed here without language and with Mexican skills and education. They operated portable corner food stores from the back of trucks or pushcarts and sold tacos and *elote* (corn) and fruit. The women became seamstresses and communion dress designers."

"Today these pioneers have turned their corner business into grocery stores and tortilla factories, clothing stores, and restaurants. When we renew their memberships they want us to come and visit the store, to have lunch, to sip tea. They want the personal touch! They are proud; they want to show us the facility.

It is a different generation and I know one approach does not work for both."

Martha continued, "I live in a hybrid world." As she said hybrid world, I gazed out the meeting room window, which overlooked 26TH Street. On one corner I saw a woman dressed for the cold just starting to sell boiled ears of corn and other lunch time treats for the various business men and women for a mere $1.25. Not far from the Señora selling the corn, a bank advertised the acceptance of *matricula consular,* and free checking accounts for new customers who may well be among Pilsen's recent arrivals.

The *matricula consular* is an official I.D. card, which is issued by the Mexican government through its Consular Offices. The document proves *only* that the bearer is of Mexican nationality and is living outside of Mexico. Many opinions surround the *matricula consular,* also called the *matricula,* which will not be discussed here. However, for more on the *matricula,* visit: www.cis.org/articles/2003/matricularelease.html.

Martha continued and her elegant voice spoke about childhood memories. "One year during grade school, when the teachers were on strike, the Alderman of the area set up alternative schooling for us. We had class. During the summer, my dad would make me translate English books into Spanish. My dad would tell me, 'Martha the culture and heritage is yours to protect, but you must also nourish it.'"

Martha asked me if I have ever been to a Pilsen parade. Her goal is to make La Villita a tourist destination. "We have culture here. We are selling culture. This village has existed for 30 years. Do you know that people from Iowa, Wisconsin, and Indiana come here to buy First Communion dresses? Bohemians and Polish people once populated La Villita. Today, as in the past, it has been an arrival point for recent immigrants. Big business knows this and they come here to attract our people. They want the benefits of the community, yet normally they don't operate within the community. Many big corporations sponsor our parade. Yet, it is as if big business thinks we should provide to them some sort of operating instructions when what it requires is two-way communication. Otherwise business owners will continue to have doubts about how to operate in this historical and charming community and they will arrive blind with misperceptions."

Unfortunately, some big businesses may still allow misperceptions to creep into advertising and marketing. According to public opinion polls for the last 50 years, Hispanics feel the images used to portray them have been somewhat distasteful. An example is from the 1920s and 1930s when Hispanics were portrayed in films as funny, sleepy banditos. This is in contrast to the way Hispanics see themselves and in stark contrast to income and education. Only recently have U.S. businesses begun to actively destroy the images of the early days.

As reported in Time Online Edition[2] (March 10, 2003), when Gigante Supermarkets entered California, a U.S. snack manufacturer's representative asked a Gigante category manager to cover any outstanding debt that the business might not pay or pay in a timely manner. This practice may be common with the many Mom and Pop grocers in parts of Los Angeles, but Gigante? Was the rep poorly informed? Did he not do his homework? Did he apply past interactions with Hispanic owners of Mom and Pops to the largest supermarket chain of Mexico now doing business in the U.S.? Not all businesses, as Martha mentioned, are similar.

I have been asked, "Is it the responsibility of the marketer and advertiser to understand the deeper significance of Hispanic culture?" Yes, certainly from an ethnic and lifestyle position. However, after digging deeper, the client most often is asking me, "Is there any universality here? I don't want to build this from

---

2 "Fresh from the Border," by Romesh Ratnesar, Time Online Edition, March 10, 2003.

scratch!" I interpret this as a search for cultural universals.

Many consultants that claim to understand the Hispanic consumer identify the major differences between the general public and the U.S. Hispanic. In my firm, we attempt to understand how an existing product or service may be of interest to Hispanics. In essence, we find ways of taking an existing product and positioning it to and for different markets. As a businessperson the last comment I want to hear about an existing product is that I have to start from scratch, that all consumers hold nothing in common, and this outreach program is about to cost loads of cash.

It is important for marketers to uncover what is common among their customers. Universal aspects of the cultural environment represent opportunities for marketers. George P. Murdoch in his book, *The Common Denominator of Culture* (New York: Columbia Press, 1945) suggests that there are commonalities such as sports, body adornment, cooking, courtship, dancing, decorative art, education, ethics, etiquette, family feasting, food taboos, residence rules, status differentiation, and trade. With this list as a starting point, the astute marketer can begin reaching towards the universals, denounce stereotypes, and realize opportunities.

As to the significance of ethnicity, interact with your customers. Whether they are Mexican-American, Cuban-American, or Latin American, they envision themselves as a distinctive people rather than as fully integrated into the American identity. They will hold certain identifying cultural values and you can learn by merely observing, then you can market to these identifying values.

Lessons from the Street

Faith as a Cultural Modifier

In Guadalajara, Mexico, working for 7-Eleven of Mexico I was introduced to faith as a positioning statement. I became acutely aware of the relevance of faith to the Mexican consumer as well as how conspicuous it actually can be.

The majority of Hispanics in the United States were raised at Catholics and their faith guides them. The 2001 American Religious Identification Survey (1)[1] found that 29 percent of this country's 50.9 million self-identified Catholics were Hispanic. Of 25 million English-speaking adult Hispanics represented in the same study, 75 percent said they were "religious" or "somewhat religious." The degree of faith is not of consequence or concern. However, what should concern you as a retailer trying to appeal to Latinos is the role faith can play in the retail environment.

In Guadalajara, for example, a new store was not complete without the blessing of a Catholic priest. The priest said Mass at the local church and gave his homily speaking of the roles these 7-Eleven stores should play in the overall well being of Guadalajara. The priest spoke from the pulpit about community, responsibility, awareness, employment opportunities, training, and guidance. He said that 7-Eleven Mexico should act as a good corporate citizen and provide to the community: product, employment, safe haven, and hope for additional opportunity for all of God's people. He was resolute in his delivery and the connection between faith and retailers' responsibilities everywhere to maintain a level of corporate respect and involvement with the communities in which they operate. When Mass ended, the dignitaries and politicians and employees of 7-Eleven Mexico and the Southland Corporation, parent of 7-Eleven, were off to the reception at our beautiful new store where the crucifix was presented and the priest blessed the store, as with many retail establishments, the crucifix was then attached over the door.

---

1 Kosmin, Barry A. and Egon Mayer, American Religious Identification Survey 2001, The Graduate Center, The City University of New York.

Faith in the U.S. Retail Context

As mentioned elsewhere in this book, retailers in Little Village in Chicago and the Gigante Supermarket in San Diego understand what faith symbolizes to their customers. These retailers stay open late and cater to their customers on Holy Days or *Dias Festivos*. The connection to faith is present. Some general public supermarkets sell *velas* or religious candles, too. However, just because your store is selling the *vela* you cannot assume the folks in merchandising understand what it is and why it sustains a need for the customer. They should. I do not suggest making your location a destination for religious zealots, but I do suggest something more than that inspirational 4x6, black framed, picture of the Eagle, wings flapping and floating in the direction of the financial Gods.

Businesses with operating structures that pay attention to the Faith Positioning Statement are businesses that may be perceived as better understanding their Hispanic customers. They may be perceived as honest or proper. Or it may be as simple a message as "It feels like home: Mexico, Puerto Rico, Cuba, here!"

CHAPTER 4

Applying the 4 Ps to the Hispanic Consumer

The Four Ps (Product, Price, Place, and Promotion) is a well-established tool to view the traditional marketing mix tools. However, you can learn a relatively quiet and not frequently discussed concept by replacing the 4Ps with a customer-based model. In the table below, the 4Ps represent the seller's point of view of the marketing tools available to influence the buyer. In his text, *Marketing Management, Eighth Edition* (Prentice Hall, 2003) Dr. Philip Kotler discusses Robert Lauterborn's suggestion that the 4Ps correspond to the customer's 4Cs.

From a buyer's point of view, each tool of the marketing mix should be designed to deliver a benefit to the end user—the consumer. Yet, how do the four Ps translate into benefits for the Hispanic consumer and more importantly, how can the Four Ps be used to attract the Hispanic consumer?

Your company may wish to establish an offer mix of products, services, and prices and use a promotional mix of advertising, salespeople, public relations, direct mail, and in-store coupons in order to reach the distribution channels and target customers. Marketers must decide on how to allocate their company's marketing dollars to the products, channels, promotion, media, and sales areas, consider direct versus distributor sales, and look at the geographic mix. To make these decisions, the marketing managers will use the concept of sales response allocation, or who and how will sales be affected by the dollars invested in each possible application or area of the product mix.

Four Ps to Four Cs

To put the customer front and center in these decisions, consider using the
Four Cs, rather than the four Ps. The Four Cs should drive the Four Ps

P	C
Product	Customer needs and wants
Price	Cost to the customer
Place	Convenience
Promotion	Communication

Source: Based on a table in *Marketing Management,* Eighth Edition, by Philip Kotler (Prentice Hall, 2003).

Customer needs and wants (Product) Product is the most basic of marketing-mix tools. It is the firm's tangible offer to the market. It includes quality, design, branding, features, labeling, and packaging. If Product and its various components are to be attractive to Hispanics, then the Customers' needs and wants must be understood and represented in the product.

Hispanics are not the general public who speak Spanish. Companies marketing to U.S. Hispanics need to understand the roles their products fill, to whom they appeal, and if they serve a different function for different cultures.

Many companies attempt to use a product or communication extension as a strategy for pursuing customers in foreign countries. They sell exactly the same product, with the same advertising and promotional aspects as used in the home country. In essence, it is a type of geographic expansion and in order for it to be successful ethnocentric similarities must exist. Thus, the producer makes the assumption that consumers in various world markets are similar, or the conditions and retail environments are similar. With the proper conditions and the correct retail environment, this method can be profitable and inexpensive.

Other companies may choose to expand or extend a product line but do not assume the consumers in different markets will behave similarly to those in the home market. These companies follow a geocentric model.

For example, Campbell Soup introduced the U.S. version of tomato soup in the United Kingdom. Campbell realized, after poor sales, that the English taste buds preferred something more bitter in its tomatoes. Campbell was incorrect to assume similar tomato soup tastes at least between the UK and its U.S. market.

In the U.S., Procter & Gamble produces Charmin Bathroom Tissue or *Papel Higiénico*. The Hispanic product is available in the United States and it is marketed in the same package, with the same graphics, but the packaging message is bilingual. Charmin maintains its Squeezably Soft!® tagline, but continues with:

- One Charmin Ultra Double Roll has twice as many sheets per roll as a single roll of Charmin Ultra

- Un rollo de Charmin Ultra Rollo Doble tiene el doble de hojas por rollo que un rollo sencillo de Charmin Ultra

In this example, Procter & Gamble is selling exactly the same product but with an additional language promoting the same appeal and product benefit.

Colgate-Palmolive, on the other hand, manufactures Suavitel, a fabric softener made in Mexico, advertised in Spanish, and carried at U.S. and Mexican retailers, large and small. Its packaging depicts a woman smiling while holding her child, and the product is promoted in two languages.

Property of Colgate-Palmolive

Sticking with household items, how about Fabuloso!, also from Colgate-Palmolive. It is a liquid cleaner or *Limpiador Liquido*, which comes in many scents. My favorite is lavender or *Fresca Lavanda*. It is a brilliant purple color, attractive to Hispanics, but also to me. I also like the product due to its cleaning ability, lovely smell, and price point at most retailers.

We have three examples of household products —bathroom tissue, fabric softener, and laundry detergent—one produced in the U.S., the other two outside of the U.S. by two different, yet competitive, manufacturers. Procter & Gamble appears to have chosen to simply translate the features of the product, and not change packaging. Colgate Palmolive, manufacturer of Suavitel, positions its product to the Hispanic. Until recently it was marketed in the U.S. predominantly at bodegas. Today it appears in the kitchens and bathrooms of the general public too.

How a manufacturer decides to enter a market depends on retailer input. The days of push-through marketing are a thing of the past. Informing your distributor or manufacturer of your changing customers will ensure that the product is built, redesigned, extended, adapted, or invented to meet your customers' needs.

Whether you choose to use shelf space for Downy or Suavitel, Fabuloso, or Spic'n'Span, should depend on the external factors of customer needs and wants and the market in which you operate, as well as your internal operating model and the payments associated with volume turn, rack and positioning payments, promotion surrounding the product, price reduction for large purchases, and desired gross profit margin.

Cost to the customer (Price) If Price is to be attractive to the U.S. Hispanic consumer, the perception of cost and value associated with the product to the customer must be understood.

Price will be discussed in some detail because it is the only profit producer in the four-P mix. It is the critical tool. Price is the fundamental in the marketing mix that provides for revenue; all other elements represent costs.

All profit-making organizations, and many non-profits, set prices on their goods or services. In a myopic sense, price is the amount of money charged for a product. From a larger perspective, price is the sum of all the values that consumers exchange for the benefits of having or using the product. Price is also one of the most flexible elements of the marketing mix. Unlike product features and channel commitments, price can be changed quickly, particularly in the short term through allowances and discounts. Simultaneously, pricing and price competition is the number one problem facing many marketing executives. Yet, many companies do not handle pricing well. The most common mistakes are:

- Prices are too cost oriented or retailers desire a certain markup on the product.

- Prices are not reviewed to reflect changes in the market or in changes of the competition. Thus the product will not move off the display.

- Prices do not take the entire marketing mix into account.

- Prices are not varied for different products, different market segments, and different purchase occasions.

Entry into a new Hispanic market may add costs to your product or product line. However, you must exercise caution here so as not to attempt to capture all the costs associated with the new market entry because it may make your product less competitive with those of other businesses that also have the product.

Promotional costs need to be built into your price. These include any costs associated with the promotion of your product such as your time conducting demonstrations and making sales presentations, samples given at demonstrations to store owners and restaurants, advertising expenses, broker and distributor fees or allowances, spoilage, non covered returns and any other costs related to the promotion, selling, distribution, and servicing of your product. Taking into account all costs including items such as sales presentations is critical because many new entrepreneurs donate their time instead of making sure they pay themselves a "salary" for their services.

There are also costs associated with the revenue collection. There are customers who will pay after their bill is due or in some cases will try to get away with not paying at all. Many customers will also negotiate a discount on paying early—such as one or two percent in the first 10 days—then pay late and still take the discount.

It is important to guard against under pricing. The price you give to a product lends a certain value to the item in the mind of the consumer. Under pricing often leads the consumer to believe that the item is of little value or of inferior quality in relation to others on the market. However, it is equally as important to guard against over-pricing your product. If it is overpriced, you will not be able to compete in the market place.

When pricing your product, you are placing a value on your product, your company's strengths, and your customer service. This reflects your understanding of your neighborhood, its socioeconomic situation, your customers, and your ability to deliver the product. You are not simply selling a product. You are selling a package, which includes the unique features, advantages, and benefits of your product, your company, and your customer service.

Hispanics want what they pay for

As long ago as 1999, an article in *Retail Merchandiser* entitled "Marketing to Hispanics: Beyond the Obvious," warned that unlike non-Hispanic consumers who are likely to follow their whims from brand to brand and store-to-store, Hispanics are more loyal to brands and don't like to give up a brand. Hispanics are more in a "needs" mode than a "wants" mode. *Retail Merchandiser* quoted Jo Musser of Mendoza Dillon, an advertising agency involved in Sears' Hispanic marketing efforts. "They're looking first for quality and durability and then price, and will save and spend to buy the best. A common misconception is that all Hispanics are non-white, low income, and non-English speaking. It is a mistake to only look at Hispanic's disposable income. Areas with a high density of Hispanics may be low-income resulting in some price limitations, but the Hispanic population living in these areas still desires good brands and high quality."

Hispanic perspective on pricing

In December 2003, a Mexican business woman in California told me, "I am interested in buying this gas station and convenience store, but I believe there to be a problem with the financial statements. My payback period is too long based on the gasoline margin contribution. I just don't understand why the gasoline margin per gallon is no greater than nine cents per gallon."

My client's perspective comes from owning and operating numerous Pemex (Petroleos Mexicanos) gas stations in Mexico. In Mexico the government sets the retail street price for gasoline, a monopoly. In the United States the retail price for gasoline is normally a function of the competition in the trade area.

Thus, a nine-cent margin in the United States versus twenty cents in Mexico is a giant difference. Even larger is her misunderstanding of the retail-pricing philosophy of gasoline and her application of Mexican pricing philosophy to American business. My client's application of Mexican gasoline margins to the Los Angeles market was incorrect.

Addressing this from the retailer's perspective, too often general market retailers make a similar mistake. They fail to understand their customers, their time in country, and country of origin, if from outside the U.S., and how this relates to the perception of price in the mind of the consumer.

In an effort to assist the retailer in setting prices for items geared towards Hispanic consumers, think about the four Hispanic shopper segments described in chapter 2 and how Hispanic consumers shopping behavior fits into each segment. The four categories do not pertain to markup and working from cost to retail, both internal functions driven by accounting requirements. Rather the categories are about understanding price as a component to the Hispanic consumer, and understanding it to be significant factor in the buying process.

To review quickly:

Economists will buy and stock sale items and be diligent about responding to advertising about sale items and specialty goods. Economists are not loyal to one store or brand.

Loyalists come prepared with a shopping list, visit a primary store, and attempt to do the majority of the shopping at this grocer.

Pricehunters shop around and are the most price sensitive.

Traditionalists are brand loyal and are not willing to risk a new brand for a proven brand. Traditionalists are the least impacted by advertising.

An illustration of how this segmentation works on pricing can be found in bottled soft drinks. These beverages are normally priced at a point that is attractive to even the poorest in the country or those just above poverty level. Thus, when Hispanic Traditionalists arrive in the U.S., their comprehension of price will be in relation to the prices they paid at home. If they are accustomed to paying the equivalent of 55 cents for a 20 oz. non-returnable plastic bottle of soda in their home countries, having to pay $1.09 or greater for a similar product at the typical convenience store, even assuming purchasing power parity exists, might present a price barrier. I understand margin is required by product, but the price difference may be exceedingly large for Traditionalists and Pricehunters, whereas Economists and Loyalists would not have to make this comparison.

As the terms suggest, Hispanic shoppers are a broad and diverse category, yet further insight suggests culture and tradition move across generations. As the Food Marketing Institute report cited earlier said, "Sixty-five percent of Hispanic grocery shoppers agree with a statement that they teach their children to prepare traditional meals and only 20 percent of Hispanic grocery shoppers agree that their children like American food over traditional Hispanic Food."

It would be wise for the bankers, auto dealers, grocers and convenience store owners, bodegas and the like to not solely look at language preference but also the opportunity these four categories may represent to your business.

In a report published by The Food Marketing Institute measuring supermarket features that were important when deciding where to shop, 92 percent of all U.S. Hispanics rank price as important. By language segment, 93 percent of Spanish-preferred, 86 percent of bilingual, and 86 percent of English-preferred, rank price as important.

I am not suggesting a different pricing structure for Hispanics in your market. What I am suggesting is that a bodega in Brooklyn may sell fabric softener for 20 to 30 cents above the average retail price found at a grocery store, but this retailer may be adding a convenience fee as well as a comfort fee for proximity and language. It is really about understanding your profit model and how not to price your product out of range for this potential customer. However, you should always keep in mind, the Food Marketing Institute finding that 92 percent of all U.S. Hispanics rank price as important.

The roles of Hispanic shoppers

Now let's look at five roles that may be involved in the decision-making process, especially if the purchase involves more than one person as it often does with U.S. Hispanics.

Earlier I mentioned how LA Motors was catering to its customers. What I didn't tell you earlier is that a bilingual 25-year-old son was assisting his parents in their decision. It did not seem as if he was influencing their choices of options or features of the car, but during the haggling process, he did go to the desk with the gentleman who appeared to be his father.

Distinguishing the role of your customer will help you understand the buying process and how to interact with each of the parties involved. Five roles have traditionally been identified:

Initiator: The person who first suggests the idea of buying a certain product or service

Decider: The person who decides what to buy, whether to buy, or where to buy

Influencer: The person who is able to provide insight into the purchase or give advice

Buyer: The person who makes the actual purchase

User: The person who uses the service or product

Retailers of all types must take note of the influencers and the initiators. A young Latina in Chicago told me that when she came home from college after her first year, she decided it was time to show her mother how to open a checking account. "I drove her to the bank. We opened the checking account and ten starter checks were handed to my mom. The bank employee continued to talk to me instead of my mom. We were speaking Spanish because my mom's English is really bad. I politely switched over to English, and said, 'My mom is the one who is banking with you, not me. Please explain checking to her.'"

As computers play a larger role in education, parents are likely to make a financial commitment to buy a computer, certainly when there is a strong influence from the children. While the parents are the buyers, the user is the child, according to a major manufacturer of computers. Often the influencer may be a friend from school who suggests a computer purchase. The parents may not know if your price is competitive, but the kids do and if your price isn't competitive, the kids will suggest making the purchase elsewhere.

Convenience (Place) The various activities the firm pursues to make the product accessible and available to the consumer. The Place must be Convenient for the customer.

Because manufacturers are in the business of manufacturing, and not in the business of distribution, companies have to undertake many activities to ensure the product is accessible and available to the target customer. It is also the producer's responsibility to identify, recruit, and link numerous and various middle sources and marketing handlers so its product and services are efficiently supplied to the target market.

Case in point: Perhaps it was because the guacamole was prepared at my table at the Santo Coyote restaurant in Guadalajara, Jalisco Mexico. Perhaps it was due to the guacamole being prepared in a *molcahete*, or a serving dish, which is made from volcanic stone. The taste was amazing, and I decided to buy a *molcahete* in Chicago. I couldn't find the dish in Chicago, so I forgot about it until I was visiting Prarie du Sac, Wisconsin.

With 3,100 residents, Praire du Sac is located on the Wisconsin River, about 45 minutes from downtown Madison. It has a grocery store, post office, and an old-time movie theater. The residents there serve hot chocolate to visitors in the month of January when eagle watchers camp on the banks of the river to watch bald eagles nest.

Little did I realize that in this largely agrarian community, I would find my *molcahete* in a bodega-type store recently opened by a Mexican family on the banks of the Wisconsin River. Like others, they had made Praire du Sac their home and were creating a demand for the common spices, tortillas, and soft drinks from their native land.

When I asked the store proprietor, a woman about age 25, why she opened a store with Mexican food products, she answered, "Because I can never find the Mexican staples at the local grocery store, so I opened my little store. We have one car in the family, as most Mexican families here do, and it is too far to travel to Madison daily for our food. Also, I don't feel safe traveling the country roads between here and Madison, so why not open this store."

Travel time, mentioned by this Hispanic consumer, may have been a dimension missed by the other retailers in the town. This suggests that Hispanics who purchase at this local bodega might be somewhat pressed for time—a qualifier of convenience.

Managers of malls, hypermarkets, and drug stores should focus also on the dimension of safety for their Hispanic customers (and others). This could be done through a variety of ser-

---

Lessons from the Street

A win-win for supermarkets, customers, and kids

More than 3.5 million children in Mexico work. Some start as young as age 12 and are forced to quit school. Often they take jobs on street corners juggling or blowing fire from their mouths, or washing automobile windows at busy intersections. These same children are 2 years below the legal limit for work in Mexico.

Of the 3.5 million children, it is estimated that 24,000 young children work as bag boys or bag girls at local and national grocery stores, receiving and working on tips or *propinas*. Their contributions often help support their families.

Due to a special legal system in place in Mexico, these 12-to-14-year-olds are able to work in Mexican supermarkets only, and only if they succeed in school. They will lose their jobs if they do not attend school regularly and earn good grades. Their attendance rate is among the best in Mexico at 95.3 percent.

Source: *Hoy Newspaper,* August 3, 2004. Supplemental information provided by The Children's Study, The United Nations and UNICEF.

---

vices, such as valet parking and electric carts, to speed patrons into larger stores.

Mall locator information can be presented in Spanish as well as in English. In the mall, store associates should be trained to be knowledgeable about the stock, able to complete a transaction efficiently, and, preferably, be bilingual. Help for customers in conveying their purchases to their vehicles might also be appropriate these days, since public opinion polls indicate that many Americans are concerned about personal safety.

In Mexico at the U.S.–based HEB Grocery stores, sharply dressed 10-to-15-year-old boys and girls bag groceries and are willing to assist all customers to their autos. Usually they are tipped a small amount, U.S. $.25 to $.50. This is an added convenience built into the HEB stores in Mexico, but you will also find it in most grocery stores there—a value-added convenience.

Communication (Promotion) The various activities the company undertakes to communicate and promote its products to the target market. This includes the hiring and training of qualified and motivated sales people. Proper promotion will reflect your company's sensitivity to culture and its desire to target this group of consumers.

In 2003 a research project exploring the buying and eating habits of the Hispanic population was conducted by a publication covering the produce industry. The results were then presented at numerous venues in an effort to educate grocers, convenience store, and bodega owners across the country. The report stated that Hispanics list the same products as non-Hispanics as the products that influence their shopping and buying decisions. According to the research, U.S. Hispanics don't consume excessive amounts of avocados, cilantro, papayas, chilis, or other products that the general public believes them to consume. While these products are consumed, these are not the products that send them from one store to the next.

Assuming the research to be correct, a grocer might believe that the promotion of apples and lettuce has just as large an appeal as promoting avocados. However, promoting apples versus chilis just doesn't do the job, either. If a grocer advertises a jalapeño, habanero, or chipotle pepper, along with apples and lettuce, it sends a subtle cultural message that he is culturally in tune to the shopping needs of the community.

If the retailer believes the Hispanic consumer will consume more apples and strawberries because they eat more fruits and vegetables than non-Hispanic customers in the U.S., two lessons need to be learned.

First, Hispanics in Miami and Houston differ and so does their fruit consumption. Thus, assuming them to buy more apples and strawberries is the wrong assumption but one easily made by the produce buyer for your organization. Instead of general consumption trends, product purchased must be based on individual and geographic preferences of your customers.

Second, while Hispanics may consume more fruit, if your store is not clean, the shelves are not stocked, and the employees are not courteous, customers will not visit your store, no matter how good or appropriate your selection of fruit.

Factors of Importance to U.S. Hispanics
In percent of those who said the factor was important

Factor	Total U.S. Hispanics	Spanish -preferred	Bilingual	English -preferred
Fresh, high-quality fruits & vegetables	97%	98%	98%	90%
Clean, neat store	96	97	97	92
Courteous and friendly employees	94	96	92	86
Low prices	92	93	86	86
Fresh, high-quality meats & poultry	91	92	93	88
Convenient location	84	86	83	80
Personal safety outside the store	84	87	78	67
Fast checkout	84	85	79	82
Nutrition and health information available for shoppers	81	86	66	47
Being active or involved in community	77	82	63	45
Availability of name brands	75	80	67	53

Source: *U.S. Hispanics: Insights into Grocery Shopping Preferences and Attitudes,* 2002.
© 2002, Food Marketing Institute, Washington, DC. (www.fmi.org)

Focusing on the promotion of the above areas will lead to long-term customer good will. Using produce as an example, the above information should inform the retailer not only to have available a variety of fresh fruit available but also to be culturally sensitive to the needs of these consumers. These customers will buy fruit in larger quantities but only if they are able to identify with their heritage once inside the store.

Chili peppers are another example. Their use varies by ethnic group. For example, Hispanics from the Caribbean tend to like sweet peppers while Mexicans tend to favor hot peppers. The peppers also vary by use. For cooking, they tend to be chopped up and used in recipes. Most Hispanic shoppers will buy more chilis in a single trip to the supermarket than their non-Hispanic counterparts do in an entire year. Therefore the price of peppers becomes a significant factor to them.

If you carry produce it is important to know what type of peppers to carry based on your neighborhood. Peppers are only a starting point. You must consider variety in product selection and merchandising. Squash, tomatillos, plantains, red bananas, and chayote are a few of the items that may be essential, again depending upon the neighborhood.

Once you have the product mix figured out, merchandise it properly. Hispanics tend to buy from bulk displays. Along with a bulk display of onions, present the green peppers and Mexican green onions and other related items to create eye catching and appealing displays.

If you bulk display yellow onions, bulk display white onions as well. Hispanic shoppers prefer white onions over yellow. In addition to attractive price points, most Hispanic consumers enjoy purchasing from bulk displays because they feel as though they are actually choosing their fruit, something which is not acceptable in many cultures, where customers are expected to ask the clerk to pick out their fruits and vegetables. I learned this the hard way.

Once while shopping for fruit at El Corte Inglés in Spain, I made the mistake of actually picking up a tomato. Can you imagine that? As I picked up the tomato, the lady in the middle of the fruit display, about sixty years old with a hair net and white gloves said "Hey, hey I will help you." "No," I responded, "I just want to test the texture of the tomato." "No" she said, as she snatched from my hands my slightly mushy tomato. I was somewhat taken aback as she set the tomato on the scale. "No, no, not that one, I want . . . . Well can you actually show me a few? I am not too sure." The point is that the customers are not allowed to touch the fruit.

Lessons surrounding produce can be transferred to other business types, because from retailer to retailer the goal is to create value for your customer and drive repeat business.

Consider a range of advertising options for promoting products to your Hispanic customers. If you decide to use print media, varied ad versions and circulars can be used and may include:

- Distinct and separate mailers. Be cautious here! While you may create the proper mailer, often times it is improperly targeted. If it is included as an insert to a newspaper or periodical, ensure the vehicle carrying the mailer is of interest to your target audience.

> "Successful and confident companies are those who meet and exceed the customers needs, economically and conveniently with effective communication."
> Robert Lauternborn,
> New Marketing Litany,
> *Advertising Age,*
> Oct. 1, 1990

- Wraps and ethnic merchandising themes. A wrap is usually supplied by the manufacturer and helps advertise floor displays, such as soda or bulk displays of chips or candy. It compliments the product, wraps around the display, is eye catching, and may include a price point.

- Ethnic offerings appearing on the front page of promotional flyers designed for your general market audience.

- As a general rule, circulars and flyers for ethnic stores are bilingual. However, if placed in one of the Spanish-language newspapers, then it should be in Spanish. Direct-to-home ads are usually bilingual if the native language speakers comprise less than 50 percent of the population in the targeted relevant area. Conversely, if Spanish speakers comprise more than 50 percent of the target then Spanish-language ads are appropriate.

- Distribution vehicles such as ADVO and Penny Saver effectively reach consumers at home, especially in markets with a high density of ethnic consumers.

- If your operation is small and independently owned, don't forget about the in-language community newspaper. This is a great vehicle when home targeting is cost prohibitive. It is also a great vehicle for weekly use.

- Large chains with big advertising budgets or independent chains may want to consider cost effective local cable television. Local radio works well also.

- Outdoor media such as billboards, bus wrapping, bus cards and subway advertising should be considered but only when they are appropriate to the market.

Here is a photo of an outdoor billboard announcing a cross promotion between Blockbuster, Western Union, and Kmart:

CHAPTER 5

Building the Hispanic-Friendly Environment

Now we are at the heart of the opportunity—creating a Latin American-friendly environment at the store level. Inherent to creating a Latin American friendly environment is the sales associate. The concept may start in a corner office, but it is only as functional as how the person with customer contact implements it. If it is implemented well, management should consider the concept and the training a success. Should gaps exist, training and education may be the answer.

Commonly, retailers feel overwhelmed as to where to start in creating a Latin friendly environment. Yet, as we saw in chapter two, the store environment is very important to Hispanics when they decide where to shop and spend money. Let's quickly look at the list of significant factors again.

According to the Food Marketing Institute, an Hispanic-friendly retail environment will have:

- Bilingual employees

- Employees knowledgeable about Hispanic products

- Hispanic products

- Bilingual store information and signs

- Bilingual packaging on food

- Foods imported from the home country

This chapter provides focuses on operations, including product choices and displays.

Where to focus your attention

Rather than being overwhelmed by having so many things to do at once, it is best to focus your attention on a few of the techniques which can bring you the most success. Although much of the discussion in this book relates to food and grocery retailing, these techniques can be adapted and used by bankers, butchers, bodegas, convenience stores, grocers, auto dealers, and most other retailers.

You may want to copy and develop this portion of the book further for your individual region, market, or store. Take notes, apply thoughts, and realize this: quantum upside opportunities exist for retailers in this area. However, be assured that with each stage of development, challenges will occur. Here are some of the challenges you may hear:

- My boss just does not believe in this whole approach. She sits in her office and thinks she knows the market but she does not.

- I want to take my product to a trade show, but I don't know how to convey my message and my product. I am also concerned with how my staff fails to interact with the potential consumer. Conversation just does not flow.

- Management resources are tight and will always be tight. This is a given.

- I can't find a vendor for the product I need.

- I work for a huge corporation and product selection is centralized rather than decentralized.

- We have a planogram and we can't change from it.

- At a bank we must mind the safety of our customers and we must minimize open conversation area.

- Investment in attracting the Latino consumer is limited and has been typically grouped along with the general public versus a unique offering.

- The data surrounding this consumer is horrible. No product movement reports are available.

You can probably add more challenges. Be prepared. The concept of ethnic marketing is understood but the merchandising techniques are not. In order to better sell your additional profit center, whether it be a complete store reset or simply the integration of an additional product line, be prepared to respond to the nay sayers. Simply ignoring the pundits does nothing for the long-term commitment required from management or for career advancement.

There are eight key areas that can help in your campaign to attract Hispanic customers. Four of them are discussed in this chapter. The other four will follow in chapter 6. In this chapter you will learn about exterior presentation, researching Latino customers, merchandising and implementation, and how to build on a store that already exists. Issues of staffing, value, community involvement, and measuring progress will be undertaken in Chapter 6.

Identifying your exterior message

Appearance sells and exterior appearance and the merchandising outside of the business may be a principal reason customers choose to shop your locations. Just think of Disney World. The fact that many communities regulate appearance suggests that it matters. In Santa Barbara, California and Barrington, Illinois, appearance requirements show the desire of city council and planning commissions to keep the environment crisp and clean. Obviously, it is important to work with these kinds of requirements rather than against them.

At the other end of the spectrum is the bodega of Brooklyn or the exotic family fruit stand in El Paso, Texas where there are no signage restrictions and no apparent building codes, just retail space. Regardless of where you are, exterior appearance sells and attracts, and should be used as promotional space to attract customers.

Arandas Tires and Rims in Chicago is a Mexican American-owned Tire and Rim specialty shop. The owner is Erny Lopez, a young Mexican-American under age 30. This specialty tire and rim store is Mr. Lopez' dream and it is the furthest from a Goodyear or Firestone store you could find. It is located on Ashland Avenue in the heart of a Hispanic section of town. What I love about this place is the cleanliness of the exterior and the message the owner sends and how he does it. The building front itself is complete glass and from the street you can see the various types of high-quality rims and wheel accessories he offers. The rims are displayed so that at night passersby can see them easily. Mr. Lopez uses different lighting to create a Las Vegas-type of effect.

Better yet are the artificial palm trees, which he had built specifically for the location. During the day they are attractive, but even more so at night when green, blue, red, and yellow lights illuminate the palms and draw attention to Arandas Tires and Rims. Who would think Chicago and palm trees, but this guy did. Customers and curiosity seekers alike call the place Las Vegas, Little Miami, and Tires and Rims on the Strip. When asked, "Why palm trees?" Mr. Lopez's response was, "Chicago is dark and gloomy and the tire and custom rim installation business can be gloomy as well. Thus, I decided to give it some color and some energy. I lived in Mexico and I like the color. I have heard it all, but what is best about it is, the customer knows his auto is in good hands. My place is clean and I don't advertise, except for on the street—The Palms!"

The perimeter is usually the first impression your business makes. If the perimeter of your store is not large, or does not exist because you are in a mall, or operate in the middle of a city, how do you use the windows? Personally, I do not favor sign, after sign, after sign, a sign for each window. It does not send a message to me. Or the message it sends suggests nothing in the store is on sale, or everything in the store is on sale, which is it? Nothing pops!

There are also safety issues here. When signs cover all the glass, employees cannot see the street nor can customers see into the store.

One retailer in Palm Springs uses his perimeter to advertise the fact that Spanish is spoken here, "Se Habla Español" and uses two window signs only. One window sign advertises a soda product in Spanish and the other sign advertises another product in English. Each month the signs and products change and never is the sign placed so as to impede vision into or out of the store.

The impact of the perimeter or exterior

The exterior of your establishment should be a call to action. The action must be inviting and say, "Come buy from me. I want your business." The use of the exterior or perimeter should be viewed as promotion space. Merchandise it, but follow these simple rules:

1. Ensure that the area is clean and well maintained

2. Determine whether a bilingual message is needed. It probably is.

3. Don't junk up the area. More is not necessarily better.

4. Poor language and poor grammar makes people laugh, but not necessarily purchase.

5. Windows and doors should be well maintained. Any advertising space should be sold to vendors, not just provided to them, especially if it is a new or introductory product.

This window sign is from a KFC. Proper language, price and value are indicated and easily seen by the consumer from the street as well as upon entry

Note: Price is in Mexican Pesos

Easy ways to research your Latino customers

To uncover the preferences of your Latin American customers you need research. Retailers who understand how to identify their customers are better equipped to market to them successfully because they show a sincere desire to serve their customers' needs.

The process of identifying your customers' needs begins with time spent with customers, at the library, on the internet, with the chamber of commerce, with the vendor or manufacturer, or even in the country of origin of your predominant customer. Rick Bayless, the restaurateur I mentioned earlier, travels to Mexico to understand the tastes, available ingredients, and the culture surrounding food and food preferences. I suggest using a combination of such knowledge as the above to make decisions surrounding product selection, language, staffing, and marketing. I suggest using several different methods:

- Visit www.census.gov for demographic information on your area.

- Join the chamber of commerce in your area. Some cities have a special chamber section for Hispanic businesses. The United States Hispanic Chamber of Commerce has an easy-to-use directory of local Hispanic chambers at www.ushcc.com.

- Attend a Catholic church event in your neighborhood in your trade area and attempt to identify your customer base. Take a bulletin at the end of Mass. Is it bilingual?

- Drive your trade area and look at non-competing businesses. What are they doing to attract the Latino consumer?

- Eat dinner in a Mexican, Cuban, Salvadoran, or other Latin restaurant. How are the dishes different? How do the customers pay? How long do they sit?

- Mystery Shop competitors especially popular providers in your area. For example, if you manage a bank and Banco Popular, known for its Latino outreach program, is in your area, then do the following:

  1. Observe the banking experience.

  2. Inquire about the products being offered, hours of operation, language of associates, etc.

  3. Watch the interaction between employees and customers.

  4. Find out if the establishment has a customer service department and whether information is in both Spanish and English.

5. Check location sign and language.

- Go to the internet and type in key words surrounding Hispanics and preferences

- Look to national well-known companies for guidance; in other words, benchmark. What are companies like Goya and Sears doing to compete for this customer?

- For food and related food products, look to your distributors for up-to-date product information, hot sellers, and new products in the category.

Regardless of your product, you need tools to understand how to relate to your Latino customers. Better understanding will help minimize the risk associated with new products and new consumers. Your research initiatives will demonstrate your interest in reaching out to this market.

Deciding how to best serve these customers

Consumption behavior is a good indicator of type of product that should be offered. An imperative question all retailers must ponder is: "Based on time in country, how acculturated is my customer base?" or, "To what extent have my customers adopted to the life in the United States and more specifically, my neighborhood?" Studies show that immigrants who have arrived in the last 10 to 15 years are not anxious to adopt mainstream American culture, especially if it is at the expense of their own culture. Conversely, they will adapt and modify according to products found in this country. Savvy retailers will use this strategy to develop and mold their merchandising strategies.

In deciding how to serve these customers, if at all, the retailer should realize one thing: In general, the more options available to Latino consumers in a given market, the greater the effort a mainstream retailer must make to become a legitimate substitute shopping destination for this consumer.

The following chart may help you identify various approaches, ranging from a general market store to a multicultural store to an ethnic store. The Hispanic customer in your neighborhood will help you shape positioning, approach to marketing, category management, product assortment, merchandising, distribution, and sourcing.

	General Public Store	Multicultural Store	Ethnic Store
Positioning	Secondary store—emergency shopping	Primary store—daily shopping	Primary store—Latin food choices, secondary store for non-food products.
Approach to marketing	Not extremely adaptable to Latin American needs	Adaptable to a Latin American product introduction	Latin American presence is felt in all areas
Category management	Guided by high volume movement across the chain	Willing to assess and find a fit for Latin American products	Guided by high volume across the chain
Assortment of product	In touch with mainstream consumer; may offer some ethnic products, but in general ethnic brands and labels are limited	Balance is key! National brands can co-exist with Latin brands; but understand where product crossover occurs	Stock and selection of product is a function of Latin American needs; ethnic labels are present.
Merchandising direction	Shaped by the management and is tough to change.	Will adapt based on need and will be instituted on a site-by-site basis	Built towards Hispanic consumers
Product source and distribution	Most likely served by a major distributor	Use of distributors on a selective basis as well as direct store distribution when required	Distributor, direct store and private manufacturers.
Example of stores	Major supermarkets, corporate-owned and operated stores	Smaller chains—less infrastructure and red tape	Adaptable, may be Hispanic owned and operated

Source: Adapted from *Grow with America*, © 2002 The Coca-Cola Research Council. Used by permission.

As an example, a fully ethnic store will:

- Serve as the primary store for most Latino grocery needs.

- The marketing approach inside the store will feel ethnic in its presentation.

- Category management, if it is a chain, will be consistent from store to store, thus offering the same product from store to store.

- Merchandising direction will gravitate towards Hispanic likes and preferences and be specifically built for this consumer and will most likely be managed via standardized plan-o-grams.

- The retail unit will be served by distributors for mainstream products, but will also be served by those with specialty products.

When you uncover the needs of your Latin American customers, you will

- Show a sincerity towards your consumer

- Assist with product set and merchandising

- Minimize poor product selection

Stand-Alone merchandising

Stand-alone merchandising is better known as a store-within-a-store approach, or in a general market grocery store, it may be a complete aisle of dedicated space for Latino products.

The merchandising of Latino product in this manner is unforgiving in that you have decided to clear retail space for a new product line. I would assume that, prior to implementing this plan, you have a firm understanding of the sales required to replace the previous product revenue as well as the support required from vendors for this to occur. Intrinsic to the success of this stand-alone approach is execution, presentation and full-shelf presentation.

One of the benefits of the stand-alone approach is that it sends a welcoming message to the Latino consumer and may breed interest from the general public consumer as well. However, the stand-alone approach or store-within-a-store may keep some Latino consumers from shopping the entire store. Most stand-alone approaches contain items such as soda and juices, rice, beans, regional breads, tortillas, canned products, noodles, sauces, and other Latin staples.

Integration of product

Integration of Latino product is the approach that retailers use when they wish to enter the market slowly. The products may be Latin in nature or Latin branded, but they are integrated among the other products within their categories. An example of this approach would be various Mexican-preferred peppers being integrated among the fruit and vegetable section or canned sauces such as Herdez brand integrated among other similar products. This approach allows the retailer to carry the product and drive sales based on research and brand preference. Another advantage is that it does not require a full stand-alone approach, but rather reduces another line or the number of facings of a competitive brand.

Integral to both approaches is guidance from management at the store. I would not leave product selection to sales associates. Rather I suggest that a manager oversee the relationship among the operators and the merchandisers and the category managers. With this approach, the operators are operating, the merchandisers are ensuring product is properly presented and advertised, and the category managers are working with the buyers helping them to decide what is and what is not needed. Simply stated, the category manager should be accountable for knowing the local market and the concepts while ideas and experiences should be passed along from him to the management in charge of purchasing decisions.

While both approaches may prove successful, two questions need to be answered for the stand-alone strategy:

- Should it have its own profit and loss statement?

- Should a category manager be assigned to it and it alone?

Methodology of merchandising

The successful retailer or specialty storeowner may have managers attend trade shows, work with providers, and design a strategy. However, without execution by store-level personnel on a daily basis, all the strategy design is worthless. Store-level personnel should execute and senior level personnel should manage strategy. In essence, it is about communication between these two groups, but often management makes decisions without input from those closest to the customer, the retail manager, and staff.

The following are some thoughts as to how to improve communication or set new expectations for communication between field level personnel and store management, whether you are using a stand-alone or an integrated strategy.

• *Define the role of a Latin merchandise set and Latin category management*

Profitable retailers can use traditional category management as a basis, but they must modify the approach based on need. Input from the store manager on price points, product selection, product movement, and even merchandising is extremely valuable. Expect your retail managers to substantiate their decisions based on interaction with the customers, product movement, and the competition. If you are introducing one new product, use this product to discuss how other products may be introduced and why the need for others may exist. Does a product you have introduced come with a category index and penetration data to determine what sells and what does not? Your manufacturers and brokers should know this information and it in turn will help define selection and activity of the chosen product

- *Shop the store to understand the activity in real time, because often the data from the manufacturer or broker does not reflect the local market.*

Latin product must be monitored regularly. "Regularly" will be defined by management, but if it differs from other categories, make sure the team at the store understands this. Profitable operators use daily sales numbers to identify products that are moving and those that are not, those that should be expanded, and those that should be deleted.

- *Set a goal for the product or the category.*

Without a goal, you have nothing to measure. Simply asking, "It is going up or down? Are sales slow or have they picked up?" is not sufficient. Set a measurable goal. How is the product selling in comparison with the other products in the store or in relationship to the number of customers. Here's an example: At a small sporting goods store in Chicago, a retailer sells *fútbol* jerseys for Mexican teams. He scans all of his jerseys in upon arrival, and then of course they are scanned at the time of sale. This system allows him to look at the scan data for the jerseys and provides him with real time information to identify what is selling and what is not. More importantly he told me, "Where I operate, all the people are Chivas fans, a well-known *fútbol* club in Mexico. Those jerseys are selling, while other teams' jerseys are not. I have too much inventory of other teams and on my next order will cut back on non-sellers and increase on Chivas related items."

• *Know the competition.*

Are the field teams and store teams aware of the competitive activity related to the Latino products? If so, is this information making it back to the management? Shop the competition for pricing strategy, assortment, new product penetration, and customer composition. These are good indicators for performance at your own store.

Segment your stores

If you are a multi-store owner or a national vendor, by now you know that different ethnic groups exist in different areas. Thus you need customized offerings.

Here are some tips to help you segment stores based on local demographics.

1. Drive the market to understand lifestyle habits of your potential customers as well as the type and number of competitors.

2. Use census data to identify the population density and composition of the ethnic groups in the trade area.

3. Perform steps one and two for each area in which you operate.

4. Identify two types of stores: Let's call them Group I and Group II. Each will be designated as a function of Hispanic population density.

   Group I – Stores with a Hispanic composition of more than 40 percent of the trading area.

Group II – Stores with a Hispanic composition of 40 percent or less of the trading area.

The data on Hispanic composition can be obtained from the United States Census Bureau as well as from several different private sources. With it, you will be able to merchandise every store based on the trading area in which the store operates. Understanding demographics will help determine what will sell and it will take much of the guesswork out of the decision.

Build on existing store experience

You need to build on your existing store experience to complement what you currently have in place, as well as adding to it. Developing the offering or the proper selection of assortment is a process. Flexibility and willingness to change and modify is important. Stay open minded. This is the opportunity to experiment with new concepts, ideas, and products.

Identifying product assortment

Offering the correct product assortment is mandatory, followed by a merchandising effort that communicates effectively, addressing the needs of the Latino consumer.

Merchandise components for food should include:

- A wide selection of fresh fruits and vegetables

- A wide and appropriate selection of meats

- Everyday cooking items

- Food displays that are within customers' reach allowing the food to be touched and felt

- Competitive retail pricing according to ethnic sales volume

- Service based on the needs of your customers

- When experimenting with Latino brand categories, add to

your existing product but do so by adding a brand that is readily recognized by your Hispanic consumer. Consider products such as rice, sauces, canned juices, fruits, and vegetables, corn products, flour, soft drinks, candy, and spices.

- Some brands available in the U.S. that may be recognized as authentic by numerous groups of Hispanics are:

Badia	Faraón	Juanitas	Pilon
Barrilitos	Gamesa	Jumex	Productos Maya
	Ganzito	Knorr	Tabasco
Bimbo	Goya	La Cena	Tampico
Bustelo	Guerrero	La Costeña	Topo Chico
Cacique	Herdez	Maggi	Vitaroz
Doña Maria	Iberia	Maseca	
Duvalin	Jarritos	Nestlé	

Some of these brands may be available only in certain regions and not throughout the entire United States and this makes sense. What many manufacturers of Hispanic brands realize is that their products may cater to a certain ethnicity and culture and therefore be quite regional in their distribution and use.

Knowledgeable retailers will choose brands and product based on research of their local markets. However, Latino brands are not the sole key to success. Many international and U.S. brands are popular across Latin America. To immigrants, this means predetermined preference and familiarity with a recognized brand.

Thus, the lesson here is to insure internationally recognized brands or those brands recognized in the home country are carried at your store. Some popular food and non-food brands are shown in the table at right (left).

Companies like those listed build the offering around numerous traits including flavor profile, lifestyle preference, and packaging to attract the preferences of international consumers and will regularly import these brand elements to specific markets in the U.S. Retailers in large ethnic areas should have no problem in obtaining these products. In smaller markets, additional research and resources may be required.

Merchandising components

Three of the most critical food products to carry at the supermarket are: produce, meat, and bread. If you manage a convenience store or corner store, rather than a supermarket, you should consider how you can incorporate these or similar products into your current business. I don't suggest entering into the meat business if you are not in it, but hot food offerings and grab-and-go-type food, such as pre-prepared empanadas, tacos, burritos, churros, and regional sandwiches may be a potential profit source.

Produce

Nancy Tucker Vice President of Global Development for the Produce Marketing Association spoke to the ANTAD convention in Guadalajara in 2004. From her and others in the largely Mexican audience, I

learned the following key points:

- Our friends south of the border think Americans are fat and out of touch with fruit.
- Preferences in fruit change.

- The government of Mexico is behind a national campaign supporting five servings of fruit per day.

- The category is growing. In the U.S. alone, there were about 343 Stock Keeping Units (SKUs) of fruit and produce in 1994. Estimates are that 625 SKUs in fruit and produce will be offered by 2006.

- Merchandising is critical.

- Color, texture, and freshness are critical to any display.

On the streets of Los Angeles, San Diego, Miami, Denver, Chicago and many other cities across America, immigrants peddle fruit in the neighborhoods in which they live. They merchandise it from the back of an old pick up truck with a handwritten sign on the side of the truck (often indicating the name of the family). It is usually seasonal: watermelon, tomatoes, corn, and so forth. You pull up your vehicle, and touch, smell, and shake what you want while the proprietor sits under a blue canvas listening to native music. Correct change is appreciated and *Hasta Luego* is usually the parting comment. Fruits and vegetables are paramount to success and the critical factor is supplying the proper produce for your consumer.

Merchandising

- Don't run out of product. It sends a bad message and it will send your customer to another store.

- Offer waist-level displays, usually larger in area than for non-ethnic offerings.

- Bulk display produce and let customers know the country of origin. That is, merchandise the product professionally in the crates in which it was received.

- Offer a variety of products. The increase in SKUs is driven by consumer demand, regional preferences, and changing consumer habits. I asked Nancy Tucker what is driving the increase in SKUs. She said, "New desire for variety, new freshly cut offerings such as baby carrots and bagged salads, cross merchandising efforts, and non-perishables." Many of these new products will come from outside of the country because U.S. farmers choose to use their soil for more productive purposes. It makes sound economic sense, especially when viewed in the context of Comparative Advantage.[1]

- Close to each scale in your department, have a fruit and vegetable book listing all fruits and vegetables. It is a nuisance when the customer has to wait for the one torn and tattered product book in the store. Worse yet is to have to search for it. Does the customer base warrant translating your listing book into Spanish?

- What about a conversion chart from pounds to kilograms? Make it easy for your customer.

Quality

- Freshness, freshness, freshness! If you don't have a system in place verifying freshness, you are not in the produce business.

- If you buy a lower-grade product, less fresh, closer to maturity or expiration, then you are assuming the Hispanic consumer is value-driven rather than quality-driven. It is either top grade or it is not. Even worse would be to differentiate product quality by consumer ethnic group. This could cause irreparable harm to you relationship with your ethnic customers.

---

1 The Theory of Comparative Advantage suggests that countries should specialize in the production of goods and services that they can produce most efficiently. Thus, a given country may have a comparative advantage in the production of fruit, whereas another one might have the advantage in producing beef.

Price

- Pricing may be a function of how fruit is positioned and purchased. Is fruit an attraction to the store?

- Price accordingly and competitively. Expect lower margins but high turn rates on fruit.

- Sell the fruit and vegetables in multi packs or in multi units to suggest pricing value.

- Don't have too many pricing structures. Sell by the pound, the half-pound, or the piece.

- Remember, produce is an every day product for Hispanic consumers and they will know if the fruits or vegetables of their choice are priced like everyday products.

An excellent option for Convenience Stores

Smaller refrigeration unit accommodates day to day needs for Latin consumers. Note the bilingual advertising

Meat

Across Latin America and Spain there are *carnicerias*. These meat stores are similar to our old-time butcher shops. The meat department is important at the supermarket. Stores that cater to the Latino consumer sell a significant amount of meat as part of their daily sales.

Merchandising

- Merchandise and sell Hispanic consumers' meat preferences right next to the non-Latin cuts. You may have to expand the meat service area to accommodate a larger variety of meats. Note that meat preferences will vary by Hispanic country of origin.

- Offer pre-cut selections and recognize that Hispanics generally prefer to have meats cut thinly

- Spaniards and Mexicans enjoy their sausage or chorizo.

- Seasonal needs or holiday needs such as whole goats, whole pigs, or whole fish may be needed.

- Offer prepared meats such as fajitas, or marinated meats. Be careful to use spices that are consistent with consumer tastes, such as Cuban versus Mexican.

When I worked in Mexico, at the beginning of the year we established a marketing and promotional calendar for each region. On the calendar we noted national holidays, saint days, festivals, sporting events, and internal events that might need special product and merchandising attention. This, in turn, helped us plan for those special events where we could expect an increase in sales across all stores.

Quality

- High quality is of utmost importance.

- Freshness and sanitation is demanded. A focus on sanitation was part of a

marketing campaign by 7-Eleven in Mexico to differentiate itself. 7-Eleven spent millions of dollars to educate
employees and install the proper washing, rinsing, and sanitation equipment at all stores. All employees were
instructed to handle all prepared food with clean plastic
gloves and the marketing campaign advised our customers
of this undertaking. There has to be something to this.
Whereas in Mexico quantity of product often superceded
quality of product, in Chicago at a Mexican meat market,
in large letters in both Spanish and English immediately
behind the scale was this sign: "All our meat is inspected
by the USDA and handled in accordance with both Federal and Local law."

Pricing

• It must be competitive.

• Each product must be clearly priced.

Service

• The butcher must understand the product and cut preferences of your consumer. Hire accordingly.

• You can also serve your customer by cross merchandising
or adding products that compliment each other. Adding
cooking tools such as *metates, molcajetes, molinillos,
comals, ollas* (bean pots), *tomaleros* (tamale steamers),
chili pepper grills, and Mexican tortilla holders, among
others is an area of added profit and may reduce the number of trips to competitive shops your consumer will have
to make.

• If meat is not your forté, then perhaps an expansion to your
ready-to-go food or hot-food area is in order. Many convenience stores would be wise to investigate convenient hot

foods desired by this consumer as well as condiment areas consistent with their needs. Offering hot foods which have authentic tastes as well as offering deli meats such as ham, sausage, and roasted chicken could be a winning strategy.

Bread or Tortillas

If you have never stopped in a Latin bakery, I suggest you do so. Just walk in, pick up a tin tray, a set of tongs, and serve yourself. When you are finished, take the product to the counter, have it counted, and weighed and seek out a place to enjoy your treat. I don't suggest you install ovens and begin baking. However, I do suggest that you establish a relationship with the local Latino baker and partner with him. Bring the product into your store; let the consumer know you have it and who is baking it. Bakery offerings are popular among Hispanics. In the homeland they are priced competitively and available fresh daily. Fresh cookies, tortillas and sweets are normally separated in the store. Often these products are made in-house and can be a big draw for most Hispanic ethnic groups. Tortillas, *pan dulce*, *bolillos*, and *palanquetas* are popular but your selection and mix will vary based on Hispanic concentration and country of origin.

Merchandising

- Food 4 Less, a grocer, offers extra and distinct display cases for its bread and cakes. I suggest this approach.

- Staples such as tortillas should be merchandised near the bakery.

- Fresh individual bread should be merchandised in bins and readily available after 8:00 a.m. for afternoon and evening consumption.

Quality

- Most Hispanic grocers carry bread baked by local bakers.

- Ensure its quality.
- Ensure the producer of the bread is noted. Often previous relationships have been established with consumers in the neighborhood
- Encourage your provider to deliver frequently.

Price

Most grocers leave the suggested pricing to the bakers for breads, recognizing that bread is an item that is purchased daily. However, specialty items such as cakes and cookies are priced accordingly.

Assortment

- Hispanics tend to prefer white bread.
- Cakes and desserts are usually impulse items, so they should be prominently displayed.
- Desserts vary widely by Hispanic country-of-origin and region.

This display photo was taken at super market in Miami

The position of the display was at the entrance which suggests: Latin Pastry is here and we are in the business of attracting Hispanic consumers

CHAPTER 6

Store Presentation, Community Involvement, and Staffing

Beyond fresh high quality fruits, what other features rate as very important to Hispanics in deciding where to shop for groceries? How about where to bank? In an earlier chapter, I noted that a report published by the Food Marketing Institute found the following five features were important to U.S. Hispanics:

Fresh, high-quality fruits and vegetables 97 percent

Clean, neat store 96 percent

Fresh high quality meat and poultry 91 percent

Low prices 92 percent

Convenient location 84 percent

This rating is quite similar to that of the general public. Note, however, that 84 percent of all Hispanics also noted convenient location as important.

Let me leave the food industry temporarily and begin with an example from the world of banking. Many banks understand the need to cater to the Hispanic consumer. Bank of America has a fully bilingual website. Harris Bank of Chicago has Spanish-language ads, and many other banks are making it more convenient for Hispanics to bank. They have increased their lending for Hispanic businesses and made it easier to transfer money to Mexico. They have introduced new products geared to Latin customers, hired more bilingual employees, and introduced Spanish-language marketing literature and education programs.

They have added Latin-themed décor to their branches and even play appropriate Latin themed music in the background.

Wells Fargo is a good example. Wells Fargo was one of the first banks to cater to the loan needs of Latinos, beginning its effort in 1997. The California Hispanic Chamber of Commerce named Wells Fargo the corporation of the year because of its work in this area. In an effort to attract more Hispanics, Wells Fargo of San Francisco modified the internal color scheme of retail branches that exist in primarily Hispanic neighborhoods. In addition, it hired bilingual employees and even installed longer benches for Hispanic children who tend to make the trip to the bank with the parents. So while the parents bank, the children sit and color in the coloring books, also provided by Wells Fargo. Not only convenient, but *muy intelligente.*

How to improve the in-store experience

Regardless of the type of retail you represent, improving the in-store experience starts the moment after your customer decides to enter your store. Hence, a number of techniques and practices are appropriate and practical.

- Make sure the customers' native language is represented at the store in both spoken and written communications.

- Bilingual signage is a must. Place it at the entrance, at the exit, above aisles, on top of gondolas, at the restrooms, and certainly at checkout. You may want to make a list of the locations where you feel it is appropriate for bilingual signs to be placed at your store.

- Employee name badges with language capability noted will take the guessing out of the conversation. On American and other airlines, for example, employee badges carry the flags of the countries whose languages they speak.

- Music selection, if played, should create comfort and should be familiar to the customer base, yet not offensive to the general public. Retail studies have shown proper music can add to the experience. Red Lobster, the restaurant chain, uses music which supports its beach, nautical theme by playing artists like Jimmy Buffett and Gloria Estefan. Again, the connection is that it must compliment the environment.

- Make general announcements over the intercom in both languages.

- Solicit customer feedback and interaction in the preferred language of the customer.

As for those customers who are not accustomed to hearing another language at the store and seeing different products at the store, listen, and continue to keep focus on both the general public and your Hispanic consumers.

Connecting with the community

The best example I have seen of connecting with the community is during the Posada in Chicago's Pilsen neighborhood—the re-enactment of Mary and Joseph's search for shelter prior to the birth of Jesus during the advent season. Business owners stay open late, line the streets, and provide treats for the entire young caravan traveling behind the two community children chosen to portray Mary and Joseph.

It is this type of interaction that will display a sense of community and understanding of culture and values of the Hispanic consumer. Here are some other ways to connect with the community:

- Become a member of the chamber of commerce for your area.

- Provide education for your staff about culture and values of the consumer.

- Develop partnerships with community leaders and other business owners.

- Work with local churches.

- Develop scholarship programs.

- Hire employees from the community.

- Visit high schools and encourage youth to work at your place of business.

- Clean up the neighborhood.

- Allow fundraising in parking lots. It builds community involvement as well as a new customer base.

- Offer recycling depositories.

- Allow police to use your business as sub stations.

- Sponsor, sponsor, sponsor.

- Have job fairs.

Make connection with the community part of your lifestyle. In order to establish credibility within the neighborhood, retailers must advance beyond just charitable sponsorship. You operate in a community, and you should become part of it. You really have to be present and provide opportunities for the community as well as to local minority businesses and their leaders. Community involvement is also a vehicle thorough which you may be able to recruit employees.

Just as you have an operating plan for your store, at the beginning of each year you should chart out how and when you will be involved with the community. In establishing a plan, you set the example and the members of your staff can also be informed regarding their roles in the community. Connecting with the community is the responsibility of every single employee within the company, but the senior person sets the direction. Every employee should have a clear vision as to his or her role and place within the community.

Communicating value

What value is associated with your offering? It is not sufficient to build the store, staff the store, merchandise the store, and expect the customers to continue to return. A very real and existing value also must be represented in your store. Value is defined as the consumer's estimate of the product's overall capacity to satisfy his or her needs. Just what value your customer receives depends on how you meet her needs. In return for creating value, loyalty is built. And loyalty translates into increased customer count, increased visits, and increased profits.

Underlying this profound value statement is the fact that not all customers are equal. Companies may tend to think Hispanic customers have similar needs and wants, but we know this is dangerous and acting on this belief will in effect deplete value because of mediocre service and less-than-average offerings. Successful companies will concentrate on differences, not just on averages or demographic tables.

Marketing vehicles to touch Hispanic consumers

The value associated with your offering is contingent upon how your customer views what it is you sell as well as how you sell it. The effort to create enough value to touch or reach the Hispanic consumer must be proactive and adaptable. It really has to be current with the state of the industry, especially for those who have migrated in lifestyle to mainstream America, or acculturated. Change may come in many forms. Internal change may be driven by a change in technology, and it also may change the way in which your associates interact.

For example, technology such as scanning can reduce interaction with customers. I have had a young clerk scan items while she was on the phone and, without one word to me, point to the monitor to tell me how much to pay. I couldn't see the small print, but she didn't care. Technology can alienate customers if it is not used properly.

Other changes may arise due to shifts in the economy or the neighborhood. Thus, being fluid and proactive is key. Value for some Hispanics may be a function of their love of family, faith, food, sport, or fashion. It might be created through convenience, price, product quality, or selection.

Practices that will help create value for Hispanic consumers

- Be proactive, be a change agent, stay abreast of global news and local news

- Don't become a commodity. Brands come and brands go.

- Stress product, service, hours of operation, the value associated with your offering.

- Employ different means to promote products associated with your business.
    1. Express content and value to your Hispanic customers by your choice of advertising options.
    2. Use separate and distinct mailers.
    3. Wrap product displays in bilingual themes and concepts.
    4. Consider in-store promotion of items and testing stations.
    5. Announce special offers in local community newspapers. Also use them for advertising.

- Provide an area in your store for customer feedback. Promote customer feedback by offering free immediate gratification items in exchange for information from customers

—a free key chain, or a cents-off, or two-for-one coupon. The key in this area is to focus on listening and understanding.

- Via promotion and advertising, ensure all messages are inclusive and pertinent.

- Flourishing retailers will build promotions that portray the lifestyles, attitudes, and dreams of their consumers. Explore daily routines, interests, and family dynamics to help build these promotions. Many retailers focus on children because children are often the central focus on immigrant families. For example, photos in many Gerber baby food ads suggest the inclusion of people of color who love their children and prefer Spanish. The featured product is Gerber Baby Food, but the message conveyed is one of guidance and trust, built on instruction through three different stages of a child's development. Sure, Gerber produces baby food, but it is selling trust and nutrition. This is the value statement.

- Target specific Latino holidays and celebrations.

   Know the high-traffic and pertinent events on the calendars of Hispanic consumers. These significant events in the life of the Hispanic usually cross generations and are often cause for celebration. Events like Cinco de Mayo and Puerto Rican Independence days are large-scale events and should be recognized.

   More important is co-mingling retail opportunities and the community initiatives surrounding the event. You can bring the customers into your store, but you can also provide them with free parking for parades or complimentary product samplings on event days. As mentioned earlier, at the beginning of the year establish a weekly calendar which displays all festivals, holidays, election days, soccer matches, vacation days, etc., by company, by region, by market, by store. In doing so, you express your knowledge of the marketplace, but also your sincere interest in what is important to your customers.

- Lastly and perhaps most important, neat, crisp clean uniforms for all employees sends a message of professionalism and courtesy.

Staffing

I was at the well-known retailer, Marshall Fields, prior to the Christmas holiday and I watched a young man who was well groomed, well dressed, and well spoken inquire about a stocking job. I was impressed with how well he presented himself as well as the seriousness with which he took his first encounter. It saddened me to watch him walk away when he learned he needed to fill out the application via the computer rather than by hand.

The significance of a diverse staff

The diversity of your staff will reflect how you relate to the community in which you operate. It will allow you to market, merchandise, and add value as a participant in the community versus merely as s servant to the community. Recognizing diversity in staffing also helps to soften the "us-versus-them" mentality.

Staffing is no joke. It is your staff to whom you entrust your business and it is your staff that builds the connection to the community. Your staff must resemble the faces and lifestyle of your consumers. Diversity at your store should represent more than a color. It should be fully inclusive in terms of age, race, sexual orientation, or religion.

As to the benefits, I will list a few, but take out a pencil and add some of your own for your particular location.

Benefits

- Helps customers identify with the store. (I see a person who looks like me. I can work here.)

- Welcomes customers to this store.

- Provides vehicles for instantaneous feedback.

- Assists in the creation of a comfortable and recognized shopping environment.

- Sends a message that the retailer is a community member.

- Acts as a device to connect with the community at a non-retail level.

- Suggests a no-barrier approach to community involvement.

- Integrates rather than segregates.

- Includes rather than excludes.

- Creates a comfort level for the consumer. Here's an example from Nancy Tucker of the Produce Marketing Association. In Hong Kong, supermarkets are trying to create the same atmosphere inside their stores as is found in the fresh air markets. Employees dress similarly to those in the fresh air markets and the employees weigh, bag, and add a little extra free product as an incentive to the customer to return. As mentioned earlier, it sounds similar to the produce and fish markeet in San Francisco's Chinatown.

- Sends a message of, "We can shop here but we can also work here."

The greater the number of employees that share cultural and lifestyle backgrounds with your customers, the better your retail outlet will be perceived, and the better your customers will understand you and your willingness to co-exist and flourish together.

But, once again, the message must start at the top. At Marshall Fields, the system apparently required all applicants to fill out the application via computer. I don't have a problem with that, nor do I have a problem with pre-determined skills being required for various positions. However, what if all this kid was initially interested in was loading and unloading merchandise and learning while on the job? What is wrong with a paper application? Every corporate job I have had or for which I have interviewed, the application has always been an arduous, painstaking, hand-cramping task. Why can't hourly employees have this privilege?

We miss out on opportunities because we have systems built into our internal being. The systems, forms, formats, controls, and verifications become larger than the individuals and, in return, creativity is stunted and opportunities are missed. You drive prospects away when an applicant walks through the door and no one is available to speak to her or no applications can be located. She may be told, "We are not hiring right now." or, "Can you come back later?" or "Bilingual applications are not available." Each of these actions drives away prospects. When was the last time you applied for a position at your company? Give it a try. More lessons will be learned through this exercise than through what you may read.

I suggested to a retail client in Los Angeles that he send his son to his store to apply for a job. He did and it took three trips to get an application, a return trip to fill out an application because the previous one was lost, and a five-minute question-and-answer session ending with, "I will have to discuss you with my boss. I will call." Little did it matter that the kid was age 14, legally not able to work, and fully bilingual because no one took the time to investigate. Yet the yellowing hiring sign remained in the window.

Intelligent retailers connect with the customer via their employees. They create a customer-centered experience and in return earn loyalty. This relationship fuels conversation and innovation and allows their stores to become immediately responsible to the changing needs of the customer base. Advantages are abundant, but diversifying your staff must begin with hiring diverse managers at the field level and above. Diversity in management sends a strong message to incoming or potential employees that diversity is welcome and that there are opportunities for advancement.

The philosophy behind a diverse staff

In order to provide opportunity for all and leverage community relations to fortify employment recruitment, here are some guiding practices that you might want to follow:

- Have a person in charge of staffing by shift. He or she should be knowledgeable and available immediately. He represents the store and is accountable to your human resources manager.

- Have upper management that is supportive of store level efforts and provides on-site insight for recruiting potential employees from your pool of customers.

- Use community based organizations as excellent resources for Latin American employees. Churches, civic organization, community groups, schools, colleges, junior colleges and vocational schools offer tremendous resources for potential employees.

- Use incentives to drive employee referrals. Entice your employees to bring in reliable candidates. Research shows employees will recommend those who they feel could best represent them and are fearful of disappointing the employer. Thus they make recommendations with caution.

- Adaptability suggests:

  1. Provide resources for training and education, which may include training sessions that are in Spanish.

  2. Offer continuing education for all employees, especially English as a Second Language (ESL) courses.

  3. Explain roles and expectations of employees.

  4. Recognize the holiday and religious needs of all groups when scheduling.

Recognizing the need to hire a diverse staff means making allowances. One allowance is it may take longer and initially be more costly to hire and then communicate with employees who may not be English-preferred. However, when a retailer hires an intelligent, outgoing, well-informed person, the message sent to the community is: Shop here, work here. You are home!

Measurement

I have yet to meet a retailer who does not compare and contrast. I once worked with a man who owned a number of gas stations. He had a system in place for each of the key operating indicators, but what I loved was his pair of binoculars. Across the street from his station was a competitor and he would follow the competition's customers into the store to see if they were buying snacks and lottery tickets. Three years after my competitive friend started his business, the competitor across the street closed its doors and today the property is a used car dealership.

Introducing product measures

Much is written about how to measure movement, sales, and turn surrounding Latino products. To me, what is most important is that product movement is indeed measured and necessary changes are made accordingly.

Successful retailers certainly have measurement vehicles in place to understand how a product is moving or selling. Certainly inventory cost, rotation, inventory variation or shrink, proper retail accounting, and myriad other measurements indicate success. For our purposes here, I will deal simply with product movement.

I would never recommend adding a product to your store without answering the following questions:

- How and where will you merchandise it?
- How will it be advertised?
- How will it be priced?
- Who has responsibility for it?
- Have sales and margin goals been established for the product or for the category?
- Has an incentive been built into the sales plan?
- Has the sales plan been discussed with those responsible for the store?

After all the research is done, the products selected, and the advertising and merchandising homework complete, it is time for the product to be put on the shelf and made available to the public. My work with retailers suggests this is an exciting time, and it should be. Time, money and effort have been expended and now you want to begin to recoup your initial outlay of cash.

My advice:

- Set a goal for the category.

- Include the staff, management, and most importantly, vendors. Without the product on the shelf, you have no sales and without sales the program is useless.

- Remember each new product has a life of its own and thus a product lifecycle of its own.

A note on product life cycle: The product life cycle has distinct and unique stages in the sales history of a particular product. Corresponding to each stage are opportunities and problems with respect to marketing strategy and profit potential. If the retailer is able to identify the stage the product is in, or moving towards, then the company can formulate better marketing plans to support the product. Remember: Products have a limited life; products pass through various phases; profits rise and fall with each stage; and as products mature, different marketing, financial, advertising and other strategies in each stage of their life cycle will require addressing.

One strategy to lengthen the lifecycle of a product is to make the product new and improved at the maturity stage of the sales cycle. Thus, prior to sales declining and profit as well, adaptation and advertising and product promotion is used to keep the growth curve upward and sloping to the right, (good) versus downward and sloping to the left, (bad).

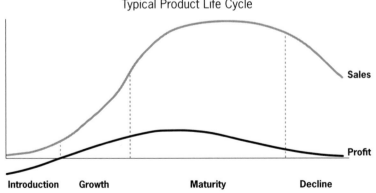

Typical Product Life Cycle

- When you introduce a new product, either with or without advertising, it may take time for the product to enter into a growth phase. Be patient. However, know how many you wish to sell per day and expect results. Note also that on the above graph, as the product is introduced, it is not immediately profitable.

- Incentive plans often work wonders in moving a product off a slow-growth position. For example, a retailer with whom I worked introduced a number of new products for Hispanic consumers. Among the products were prepaid phone cards. After receiving his initial order he informed his staff of the new product, its benefits, and gave them suggestions for how to sell the cards to potential clients. Included in his product introduction was an incentive for his employees. The incentive worked like this:

  The retailer realized about 20 percent of his products represented 80 percent of his sales. Because he carried about 2,000 different items at his store, this suggested mathematically that about 160 products were the cash cows and revenue producing products. He built an incentive surrounding the "in stock" or the availability of these 160 items on a daily basis and he did it in the form of a spot check on a weekly basis of the top 200 items in the store. Included in this list of items were phone cards.

  The retailer's homework surrounding phone cards paid off. In secretly shopping other retailers, he found them to be out of phone cards more than 40 percent of the time. After improving "in stock" of the top 160 items, he advertised to his customers: "We are in stock on phone cards or the $10 phone card is free." He paid his employees an incentive to be in stock on the most important items, with a minimum build-to level daily, no exceptions!

The above example should let you ask two important questions:

1. What is it that I must do to introduce the new products I carry to my customers?

2. Should I introduce incentives for this product category? And how?

Introducing community measures

In order to grow we need feedback. We are a country full of people wanting to know where we stand. Do you know where you stand with your multicultural customers?

Seeking feedback serves two purposes. It shows you are interested in the community and it provides a vehicle by which you communicate.

Some methods to promote feedback include:

• Bilingual feedback sheets available in store.

• Off-site paid customer intercepts give customers an opportunity to share in a safe and friendly environment.

• A feedback page on your company website. A word of caution. Remember to reply to the feedback.

• In-store "fireside chats"— a state-of-the-store and community. It is a shared meeting where information is exchanged, beverages or appetizers are served, and conversation occurs. If you are in the food-related business, have a vendor provide samples so as to minimize cost.

• Have customer appreciation days or anniversary days, and seek suggestions from the community as to how to best approach these events.

• Recognize events, promotions or significant achievements made by customers.

- Provide a community bulletin board at the entrance of the store, but be sure to approve all messages prior to them being place on the board. It allows the community and its people to be recognized as well as to share.

Regardless of the means you use, communication between you and the community is always best when it is proactive.

Customer service: Changing poor perception

Customer retention is more critical than customer attraction and the answer to customer retention is customer satisfaction. A satisfied customer:

- Buys more and remains loyal longer.
- Will purchase additional products and try new products.
- Speaks favorably about the company, its products, and employees.
- Is not as interested in competing brands.
- Will offer product and service ideas to the company.
- Costs much less to serve than new customers.

As a company realizes that loyal customers may account for a significant amount of revenue over the years, it is ridiculous to lose them over a grievance or a quarrel. Yet customers continue to come and go.

According to the Association of Hispanic Advertising Agencies (AHAA), "marketing expenditures targeted to Hispanics make up just 3.2 percent of advertising budgets, less than one-fourth the figure proportionate to their population size of 13 percent."

So could poor customer satisfaction be a larger issue, an issue that starts outside of the retail unit? It could be. Regardless of where it starts, it is your issue to address.

If you make a mistake, admit it and move on. But before moving on, take responsibility for it and put into place methodology and procedures so as not to suffer the same fate in the future.

Young market

Attracting youth is important because of their age and their current and future spending power. Because youth represents greater profit potential over a longer period of time, it is important to market services and suitable products to them. Understanding youth and having them working at your store is not only attractive to Hispanic youth, it may also sway their parents to believe in and trust the store and its products.

In designing a strategy for customer service to youth, you should reflect the actual world of today's adolescents as well as the realities of being adolescent. You should acknowledge, reflect upon, and show appreciation for what youth represents to your business.

It may be as simple as teaming up with local schools and offering scholarship programs or sponsoring youth events. Regardless of your approach, it must be seen as catering to them and built for them.

Adults

Perhaps adults are more set in their ways than children, but they open and close the cash register on a daily basis.

If poor customer service has plagued you in the past and the community is aware of it, the relationship can be fixed. To begin, create an attraction to bring back old customers—sales, markdowns, new additions to the store, a re-grand opening, or anniversary can all bring them back.

Once at the store, acknowledge their presence and by offering bilingual support for the Hispanic community. In surveys,

Hispanics have indicated selecting and continuing business with banks, insurance companies, credit card companies, and phone companies was often due to customer support in Spanish. The lesson learned here is, if you operate a service-oriented business, offer language and support in Spanish.

As mentioned at the beginning of this chapter, Wells Fargo & Co. is the nation's fourth largest bank. A 2004 (March 15) article on *BusinessWeek* online, reported that Wells Fargo adapted its branches to the Hispanic culture and offered products that cater to the Hispanic market. In answering questions about adaptation of branches and products, regional vice president of Wells Fargo, Shelley Freeman identified the following practices.

- Marketing materials are in English and Spanish.

- Employees in branches in Hispanic communities are both bilingual and bi-cultural.

- Many customers come in with their kids, so branches have long benches for the kids to wait on and are stocked with coloring books.

In describing how it adapts products to cater to the Hispanic market, Freeman explained that people other than parents and spouses contribute to the total family income, so when considering family income, the bank evaluates total family income.

These examples demonstrate Wells Fargo's effort to tailor specific products and customer service to the Hispanic customer. In doing so, they reportedly opened 250,000 new accounts between November 2001 and March 2004.

Face-to-face meetings and a handshake welcoming a Hispanic customer is of extreme importance in winning the battle. It not only sends a message of interest, but it suggests that you will make your best effort to keep this customer into the future.

Regardless of the message you choose to correct your poor image, it must be direct, humble, and contrite. Mixing the three together in-language, while pointing out the changes made, will do wonders in creating a loyal customer from one who has strayed.

CHAPTER 7

Latin-Flavored Beverages and Latin American Brands

If you are skipping this section because you don't have a beverage category, the lesson is somewhat larger. Many Latin American businesses are moving north to the United States and taking a consumer market they consider to be theirs, so while beverage may not be your glass of soda, companies like Gigante de Mexico continue to come here and do business. The question you must ask is, "Who is you competitor?"

Beverages represent significant profit potential for most retailers. Latin American companies and bottlers are positioning themselves to take advantage of the $25 billion market for beverages among Hispanics in the United States. Companies from more than five different Latin American countries and regional companies were represented at the Expo Comida Latina, a trade show exhibiting Latin food and beverages to both Hispanic and non-Hispanic consumers. Every type of beverage from beer to yogurt drinks was available at the Expo.

There were also names frequently seen in the ethnic-offering sections of supermarkets today, but which are becoming part of mainstream America. These included such brands as: Soy Fantástico, Tampico Fruit Punches, The Victoria Beverage Co. Inc., Jugos del Valle, Lifeway, and Caffe D'Amore, Inc. These manufacturers want to capitalize on the consumption and spending habits of U.S. Hispanics and they were in Los Angeles in full force.

H. Stephen Phillips, show director for Portland, Maine-based Diversified Business Communications, who has spent 12 years of his life in Latin America organizing and managing trade shows told me, "Forty percent of the vendors on the showroom floor are based in either Mexico or South America. These companies are here to market to Hispanics but also to participate in mainstream American manufacturing. They understand the U.S. market to be a strong and viable market and they have come to the Expo Comida Latina with visually stimulating displays and a certain target in mind."

The exhibit hall was packed with products positioned with words like: Authentic Mexican Product, Latino Specialty Products, Lactose Free, and Café Original. The goal is to make retailers aware of their products, then work towards the penetration of shelves, cooler space, coffee bars, and fountain machines—in-language and in-culture. Eventually, the manufacturers hope their products will be attractive to the general market. Whether products such as these have arrived at your place of business probably depends on how many Hispanics are in your market area and how tuned in to your clientele you are.

Many U.S. companies are already importing *refrescos*, as soft drinks are known in Spanish, while other U.S. bottlers, convenience store, and grocery strategists are still planning for their ethnic outreach programs or their ethnic categories. Meanwhile, bottlers rich with tradition from south of the border with names like: Jarritos, Barrilitos, and Topo Chico are penetrating the shelves of American retail.

Today with the dollar to peso exchange rate favorable for investment in the U.S., Mexican businesses need to invest less in order to do business in the U.S. Also, the North American Free

Trade Agreement (NAFTA), is creating a portal for easier trade and lower tariffs. As a result, manufacturers of Mexican beverage brands are moving into American retail to reclaim customers they consider their own.

The U.S. Hispanic customer is an attractive new source of demand for these Mexican brands. For many of the foreign brands, taking a share of market here in the States may ultimately mean survival for them at home because of extreme competition and reduced margins in their native lands. Marketers of these Mexican brands perceive this customer as intelligent and nostalgic for a taste of home. They also realize that U.S. urban Hispanic youth are "influencers." The marketing strategy is to position the soft drinks for Hispanic youth, in the expectation that the products will move into the mainstream.

Three companies Jarritos, Barrilitos and Topo Chico, all Mexican in origin, have battled for years to survive against the likes of Coca-Cola and Pepsi-Cola in their homeland. Today these companies desire a taste of America. Thus, like their fellow Mexicans, marketers of these beverage brands are banking on following the taste, flavor preferences, and consumption habits of their fellow citizens. In fact, Mexicans are among the highest per-capita consumers of soft drinks in the world, according to AC Nielsen's Scantrack service in six U.S. cities with large Hispanic populations. Latinos in San Antonio, for instance, purchased 38 percent more soft drinks than the general population.

Mexican Beverage Positioning

Managers of Topo Chico, Jarritos, and Barrillitos are targeting U. S. Hispanic customers. These brands, not common to most U.S. grocery operators, represent profit potential because they are already known to many core consumers. The companies would like their brands to be known to the general market, as well, because it is one of the largest beverage markets in the world.

U.S. Beverage Market
US $ Billions

Segment	Total $	U.S. Hispanic $	U.S. Hispanics %
Beer	59.1	7.1	12%
Carbonated Drinks	57.0	6.2	10
Spirits	40.0	5.3	13
Fruit Beverages	20.4	2.7	13
Wine	19.5	2.2	11
Bottled Water	8.8	0.7	7
Sport Drinks	3.1	0.4	12
RTD Tea	2.9	0.2	0.6
Total	210.8	24.8	12

Source: InfoAmericas

The Hispanic market is a large market with expected growth on the horizon. Mexican beverage companies are intent on attracting a new source of demand. They believe that by simply entering markets where superior profits are possible, via proper relationships, in-language and in-flavor, they will position themselves as the authentic brands to many consumers. "In essence, the misperceptions about this market place and the consumer who occupies it is to our advantage," says one Mexican brand manager. "We, the Mexican beverage brands, have noticed!"

Who is taking notice?
Big retailers

In the U.S., Wal-Mart Stores, Inc. has been one retailer that has noticed. Wal-Mart envisions itself as an ally to the U.S. Hispanic. As a means of identifying with the needs of the U.S. Hispanic, Wal-mart offers in-store tasting and trade promotions of the old-fashioned glass bottles of flavored sugar water, long carried in the motherland at the neighborhood *changaro* (mom and pop stores). Not only is Jarritos finding itself in both large and small retailers across America, it is also in both densely populated Hispanic areas and non-Hispanic areas.

Independent grocers

On a recent trip to a grocer on Chicago's Near North Side, a neighborhood once populated with Polish and Ukrainians, I found an independent grocer who imports Jarritos and Topo Chico. Lime, Lemon Lime, Tamarind, Apple, and Naranja flavors in non-returnable, long neck 13.5-ounce glass bottles occupy nine square feet of this product display, right along side Coke and Pepsi. Closer to the point of transaction is a colorful basket of different Mexican brands, with similar price points.

When asked the why he carried two different product sets of the same flavors, the retailer's comment to me was: "Those in the basket are produced here in the States and are cheaper. Thus, I am offering one Mexico homeland brand and One U.S. brand. I will watch what shakes out. I think the new arrivals will look for the Mexico homeland brand while Chicano and Chicana youth as well as urban youth will cross over to the U.S. brand of Mexican flavors, simply due to the price point." This independent retailer is on top of his game. The retailer understands he is in a changing neighborhood.

What once was, no longer is. Now, Mexicans and Puerto Ricans add to the diversity of a landscape the Polish and Ukranians call home. Note that this independent grocer does not have an ethnic section. Perhaps, he sees no ethnic groups, just Americans who happen to have different ethnic origins.

Big bottlers

Salma Hayek, a mainstream Mexican actress recently signed a contract with Coca-Cola. The actress who last year was nominated for an Oscar for her work in "Frida" will work with

Coca-Cola in trying to bridge the market between the general public and the 38 million Latinos in the U.S.

The choice of Hayek is ingenious! She is a cross-over talent, accepted and identified by numerous groups. It is Coca-Cola's advertising attempt to build on *cultural nostalgia* or to relate in-culture and in-color to the U.S. Hispanic while at the same time it reaches the general public with her massive popularity.

Transferable lessons from KOF, Coca-Cola of Mexico

The second largest bottler of Coca-Cola products in the world is Femsa of Mexico. According to Coca-Cola, Femsa, SA de CV Company "has developed its product and package portfolio in close coordination with The Coca-Cola Company." The information below shows the product portfolio for Mexico and Argentina in 1993 and the common brands to both Mexico and Argentina in 1993 with a total of 54 SKU, or stock keeping units. Note the market segment in 1993 was separated into Core and Premium segments. In 2003, Mexico and Argentina are shown once more. However the overall number of SKUs in Mexico is now 147; in Argentina the number of SKUs is 117 and two new common brands are included: Coca-Cola Light and Sprite Light.

Please note the market segment has increased from Core and Premium to Low, Core and Premium.

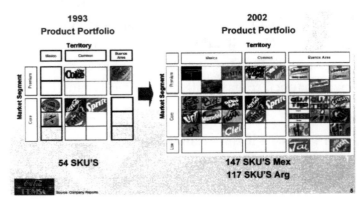

I conclude that:

- Coca-Cola and Femsa understand common tastes and consumption habits exist between Latin Americans in Mexico and in Argentina.

- A group of common products between Mexico and Argentina suggests that the core concentration should be focused on: Coca-Cola Light, Coca-Cola, Fanta Orange, Sprite, and Sprite Light.

- For these common products, the pricing, merchandising, and advertising may apply in both markets and others as well.

- Both the Mexico and Argentina markets, based on the above information, have grown in the number of SKUs positioned in each market over the last ten years.

- As the example from Femsa shows, when foreign companies come to the United States, they are quite aware of the same kind of market segmentation schemes used by domestic companies and will perform the same kind of due diligence that a U.S. company would perform if it were entering foreign markets. This example should serve as an example of the breadth of knowledge and intelligence with which foreign retailers arrive. Coca-Cola Chicago Bottler executive Bill Gallagher told me that the above common products between Mexico and Buenos Aires are consistent with the best-selling products in the greater Chicago area. What is different Gallagher said is how the Chicago bottler markets to its various consumer groups as well as the package, container, and pricing.

Recreating the familiar

Store managers need to constantly ask themselves two questions:

- What is it that my customer needs in order to feel satisfied?

- What is it that my customer desires in order to feel more at home?

"Recreating the familiar" and hoping for crossover of product from urban youth is the aim of independent grocers as well as the Mexican brands. In essence, to those familiar with the brand in their birth country it is simply taking the *Throwback Marketing Inititative.*

Research suggests Throwback Marketing or identifying with specific products in our past is on the rise. This throwback is being translated by Mexican beverage companies as *cultural nostalgia* and can be incorporated into an operating plan for your soda or *refresco* category. This has the effect of "recreating the familiar" for your consumer.

In addition to product sampling, rough plan-o-grams, and correct bilingual advertising, Mexican companies will bet on well-known consumption habits of Mexican-Americans, their love of products from the homeland and the sentiments they evoke. Recreating the Familiar also sends a message that the retailer will offer products that allow his customers a link to their native lands for themselves as well as for their children.

Remember, until recently these customers needed to make an additional stop and pay more for this product. Yet, they have been willing to do so. As one customer told me, "It has been important to me and I enjoy the taste and the message it sends to my friends when I have this product on my table."

Convenience store operators must take notice

Today the experience of concentrate and syrup producers, bottlers, and distributors in foreign lands adds to our understanding of the cultural impressions with which immigrants arrive in this country, as well as what these first-generation immigrants pass along to their children.

- In Mexico, it is not recommended to call a drink "diet" yet "light" drinks are readily accepted.

- In Mexico, fountain drinks represent a much smaller percentage of sales for soda than in the U.S. Due to relatively recent arrival of fountain drinks, problems previously worked out in the U.S. still exist today in many parts of Mexico. Thus, Mexicans who have experience with "less than wonderful" fountain drinks in Mexico may be wary of buying them in the United States.

- In numerous South American countries, mothers fill baby bottles with soft drinks when money is tight, which is frequent.

These points only serve to suggest that you should not assume you know the consumption habits of your Hispanic consumer. Ask them and depend on your suppliers for product information.

Home field advantage?

In the U.S. market, the Mexican brands are new. Marketers of the visiting brands believe culture, language, and advertising will support them. They are here to use what they know to make the consumer their own. The new brand is on the offense and moves quietly, infiltrating mom and pop stores as well as major chains, all with a fraction of the budget of the homegrown brands. The homegrown brands continue to use large budgets and large retailers and previously earned shelf and cooler space to strategically augment their market shares. The Salma Hayek's and well-known sports figures smile at us during half time of the

Super Bowl enticing us to move to their suggested brand!

Questions to ask

There are many questions retailers can ask themselves to determine if it is time to stock these new beverage products.

- Has my neighborhood changed? Will it change? Don't implement a *refresco* progam at the expense of your beverage category. This is a new brand, and you should make permanent room for new brands by understanding how these products will complement your stores as well as your product line.

- These 13.5 ounce glass bottle are tough to merchandise. Where do they best fit my store?

- What messages do ethnic offerings send to my customer? Is an ethic offering inclusive or exclusive? Is a multi-cultural approach more appropriate?

- How am I "Recreating the Familiar" at my store?

- Have I visited grocers in my area with more experience in this area to see how they are implementing their plans?

Some "Made in America" brands

Not all of the new brands are imported. Some are coming from domestic firms who are defending their territory by introducing beverages of their own. Here are some examples:

- Tropicana's Dole Beverages introduced Dole Orange Juice in 64-ounce multi-serve cartons and 96-ounce plastic jugs. The juice is available in No Pulp, Some Pulp, and Calcium varieties. Packages feature both English and Spanish text, and the product will be supported by Spanish-language commercials on Univision, according to an April 2003 report in *Beverage Industry*.

- Kraft Foods will try to stake its claim on Hispanic purchasing power with products formulated from the ground up for Hispanic palettes including a new Kool-Aid subbrand and tropical flavors under its Capri Sun label, according to *Brandweek*.

- According to *Beverage World*, Dr. Pepper used a contest, Pinta Sus Suenos ("Paint Your Dreams"), which encouraged budding young Hispanic artists, aged 12 to 18. The winner received a trip for four to the Hispanic Heritage Awards in Washington DC and $500 spending money. All winners had their art displayed on a billboard in their neighborhoods, received $1,000 U.S. Savings Bonds, and their schools were given money for art supplies. All participants had their art displayed on the Dr. Pepper Web site and received t-shirts. Dr. Pepper, for its part, has been a primary sponsor of the Hispanic Heritage Awards for 13 years.

When and how you enter this arena is your decision, but the journey should be enjoyable. However, you should ensure that you understand your consumer, prior to stocking your stores with beverages you think may sell. This is not a cookie cutter approach. The Hispanic consumer is much more varied than the generic consumer and is not simply the generic consumer who speaks Spanish! Whether your store offers *refrescos* should be based on demand and profitability!

¡Que Aprovechen! —Enjoy!

CHAPTER 8

The Role of Spanglish in Marketing

On the street we know it as Spanglish, or the mixing of native language with the newly acquired one. In the classroom, academicians recognize Spanglish as Code Switching—a way to express solidarity with the listener or to convey a certain attitude. Language purists hate it. To supporters of pure Spanish, Spanglish is nothing more than jargon and a corruption of the Spanish language. The non-purists feel Spanglish is the perfect middle ground to communicate with consumers at the urban level and beyond.

At a seminar on marketing to Hispanics, the heat surrounding Spanglish was evident. A presentation by an advertising firm included a 30-second Spanglish media bite. At the conclusion of the presentation, a well-dressed, middle-aged woman, stood and proclaimed, "I am a Latina consumer and I am offended by the poor use of the Spanish language represented in your 30-second spot. Your spot does more towards destructing our language than poor writers do in some of the most well known U.S. Spanish newspapers. Because your ad is directed at young adults, on whom we must depend for the preservation of Spanish, the metastasis becomes exacerbated. This misuse promotes what I believe is a language of nonsense. For the record, if we don't protect our language who will?"

Every day from food to fashion, television to radio, music to dance, you can see the way Spanish is influenced as well as how Spanish influences society.

- In Phoenix, Arizona for example, firefighters who take Spanish courses earn an extra $100 per month.
- Club LTV—The Latin Televisión Experience—La Experiencia Spanglish is a program about Spanglish in America.

What does all this mean for marketers in the U.S. at the retail level? One thing I have learned is that Latinos on the street, our consumers, are *chatteando* in Spanglish. On one occasion, I asked a hip-looking Chicano about Spanglish. "It is about living in three *mundos* (worlds): *Momi's*, yours (referring to the American culture) and mine. My *momi* wants me to speak proper Spanish, but I am more into setting myself apart, being different. For me and my *chicos*, (friends) it is about new identity. I speak it at lunch in the cafeteria and I use it at work. It's mine."

The retail owner must understand the reality of the target consumers, 18-to-24- year-old Hispanics. It is about understanding the dual world in which they exist. No one has truly figured it out, but this is the starting point.

Advertisers appear to have understood the message and the significance of Spanglish in business. The music industry, mass media, and the internet are also contributing to the escalation of Spanglish in America. Surf the internet and you will see terms like *chatear* (chat), *forwardear* (forward), *printear* (print) and *cliquear* (to click) from sources in St. Paul, Minnesota to San Juan, Puerto Rico, from San Diego, California to Barcelona, Spain. Spanglish has become indispensable.

Should you use Spanglish?

If you think you need or want to use Spanglish in your advertising, packaging, or other marketing communications, it may help to convene focus groups to determine what the hot points are. A skilled moderator can help you and others in your company learn how Spanglish speakers move readily between Spanish and English, creating new words along the way. Focus groups may even help you come up with some new words that are the perfect description for your product.

Incorporate ads with reflections of the lives and nuances with which Latinos are able to intimately associate. This may involve Spanglish, but a skilled Hispanic advertising agency can also reflect the culture without using Spanglish. These nuances are important and send a message of identification with the target group.

Hispanic advertising is evolving alongside of Spanglish. Borders and guidelines are blurring with Anglo campaigns and while a concept or idea can be universal, a multicultural connection must be drawn in order for it to be relevant. People from different backgrounds and neighborhoods have fun and interact with one another daily. Youth of today are acutely aware of diversity. Multicultural is now being applied to cities the general market in cities like Los Angeles, where according to the U. S. Census Bureau, 51.3 percent of the population is non-white, and Hispanics make up about 90 percent of the non-white population.

- Understand the receptivity of your audience. Not everyone will appreciate the use of Spanglish and some may actually resent it.

- Realize the ramifications and anticipate the reactions of consumers prior to roll out. If you have no idea what the reaction will be, you may want to stick to either traditional Spanish or traditional English.

- What is the role of the message? A great deal of code switching (the academic term for mixing languages together) is less concerned with what is a possible mix and more concerned with the proper conditions of code switching. Code switching is quite systematic and moreover quite normal behavior for fluent bilinguals. But if you are monolingual and think you get it, don't try it. Find a firm to assist you in your efforts.

- Most research views Latin youth as being extremely aware of and appreciative of code switching in advertising, but more receptive if lifestyle factors are used in conjunction with code switching. In other words, throwing in a Spanish word now and then doesn't cut it.

- The national marketer trying to use the same message across the entire United States may run into a mess if not first understanding the regional colloquialism of Spanglish. Major regional differences in language exist. In Miami's Little Havana, the Spanglish word for traitor is *Kenedito*. Placed in context, *Kenedito* is a reference to exiles discontent over President Kennedy's failed Bay of Pigs invasion. Thus, a *Kenedito* is significant among the Cuban population, but the word has no meaning for an Ecuadorian American.

- Standardized Spanglish does not exist. A type of *Puerto Ricanish* is spoken by Puerto Ricans in Brooklyn and it's different from the *Pachuco* spoken by Mexicans in El Paso and *Cubonics* by Cubans in Union City. And don't forget about cyber Spanglish and its world. Consequently, attempting to standardize a message for different ethnic groups may prove harmful and wasteful.

- Spanglish does not appeal to customers who prefer Spanish. It's been my experience that Spanish-preferred clientele accept me more readily when I stick to pure Spanish. It is a means of gaining their trust because they know I speak "real" Spanish and am not just trying to impress them with a few faddish words.

Gaining the trust of your desired consumer via language is only part of the challenge. Retailers of all sizes and types must understand the connotations of words, phrases, and sentence structure as well as the translated meaning in order to be confident that a message will be understood correctly.

Hallmark—Cómo se dice "cool dude" en español

Hallmark has created a line of *"Sinceramente Hallmark" cards* in Spanish. Its bilingual greeting cards combine Spanish and English words to reflect the way many Hispanics speak, communicate, and relate. This is especially true for younger Hispanics who have grown up learning and using both languages. Here are two examples of the messages found on bilingual cards at shops across America:

- Happy Cumpleaños or Feliz Birthday
- Cómo se dice "cool dude" en español

According to Deidre Parkes, spokesperson for Hallmark, "Mothers may not approve of the mixing of languages." An investigation by Hallmark revealed that the cards sell to Hispanics between the ages of 18 and 40, which substantiates Ms. Parkes' statement that bilingual cards are not for older men and women, nor for formal occasions.

In August 2004, I spoke with associate brand manager, Cindy Foley, a ten-year employee of Hallmark. Ms. Foley said, "In many ways the bilingual product was a leap of faith. Our management fully recognized the need for this line of cards and supported the initiative. The bilingual cards represent a small part of our business, while the Spanish cards are the larger part. But when you have 66 feet of cards on display at the retail level, we want to do everything we can to create success."

Ms. Parkes calls the bilingual cards, "the card for the acculturated." Hallmark held focus groups with Hispanics of all ages to determine the need for the bilingual card and came to the conclusion that bilingual cards are for peer-to-peer communication—friend-to-friend, rather than grandson to grandmother.

I have already mentioned the importance of returning to the consumer's homeland to better understand produce use, brand awareness, and purchasing habits. Hallmark did just that. Ms. Foley explained, "In Mexico, card giving is not a part of the system. One reason is the inefficiencies of the Mexican mail. Thus, we realized the lack of awareness surrounding sending cards in Mexico, and we have realized that if Mexican-Americans want to give cards, it is something borrowed from the U.S. culture."

Lessons from Hallmark? Retailers must realize Spanglish has proven effective and is another vehicle by which to reach a desired consumer. The desired consumer, most research shows, is bilingual, bicultural, and like my young hip Chicano friend shaping the tastes of mainstream America. It is the urban kid who lives in two worlds; one rich with traditional Latin values and the other youthful mainstream America. It is a group that eats hot dogs from tortillas, jumps from hip-hop to rock in Español, and watches *Friends* as well as telenovelas (prime time soaps). Management at Hallmark gets the message and supports the product.

Proceed with Caution

One of the great things about my job is that it allows me to speak, read, and write Spanish. Sometimes I do it well; other times I struggle. When it comes to translation, I leave it and the message to be portrayed to the experts. However, it is not unusual for companies to do their own translation, often using an existing member of their staff. Here are some things I have been told by clients:

- "We don't use a firm to assist us with our message. We have Cristina who is the VP of marketing and Jaime who is in the mailroom. They help us with the translation."
- "I took some Spanish in high school and what we need to translate is pretty simple. I take care of it."
- "No, we don't need any translation of message here; we used an online translation service and saved a lot of money."
- "I think we know our customers in the Hispanic market and the message we send in San Fernando Valley area of California will be just fine for our customers in New York."

My usual response is to be quiet while I am thinking, "You annoyed a lot of customers, but you saved on development costs and wonder why you see no sales." The above decisions may be correct for some firms. However a flip side does exist and my experience and research indicates that business is won and lost every day of the year because a company did or did not choose to pay attention to language translation.

We have been spoiled. With the exception of Quebec province, we have an English-speaking neighbor to the north in Canada. We go to Mexico expecting business people and vacations to be in English. Moreover, we have two oceans which until recently have acted as barriers to the remainder of the world. But times are changing.

To assume your customer or client is fluent in English is the myopic approach. Regardless of the target country or audience, language must be considered. Today, many firms still possess

Continues page 122 . . .

Lessons from the Street

The Tilde ~

The letter ñ is unique and should be held in the highest esteem, even among English speakers. To the English speaker, while it simply may be "that little hat on the letter n," it has managed to find its place, albeit inconspicuously into mainstream English. Where would stick-swinging kids of all ages be without the piñata? What would the neighborhood Mexican bar be without a piña colada?

A reference check in our own language is the *tittle* or the dot above the letter i. But is the "i" as unique as the ñ? I think not! It is unique because no language other than Spanish claims it. It also has history. Scribes used it to shorten the Latin double letter of nn in the 12th to 13th.century. Thus the Latin *Annus* became *Año* or year. It also produces a distinct sound when spoken properly; the letter ñ with the tilde placed above it is used to indicate a phonetic difference as well compared to an "n" without the tilde.

How far has ñ traveled? It was adopted in the Philippines because of three centuries of Spanish colonial rule. It is used in Euskara, the Basque language that is unrelated to Spanish, to represent approximately the same sound as it has in Spanish. It is also used in Galician, a language similar to Portuguese. While I knew it had crossed the Atlantic, little did I know it had landed in a grocery store in Northwest Indiana, an area rich with steel mills as well as Hispanics. I can hear the conversation at the sign shop making the sign. "I don't know how to make that little cap, just draw it on and put it over one of the Ns."

New Year's Day 2004, I was invited to watch college football games with some friends and family. In an effort to be a considerate guest, I decided to stop at a store and pick up some items. As I approached the store I saw a 2-feet wide by 8-feet long white sign with blue 8-inch letters hanging directly above the store's entrance:

"Coroñas-6 Pak, $5.49, Feliz Ano Nuevo!"

And I laughed over the sign's attempt to sell me a CORONA, without the tilde and also wish me a Happy New Butt, as Ano is butt in a non-anatomical portrayal. Año, with that little hat, is year.

inadequate or outdated foreign-language sales promotion materials. These same firms may move into prospective neighborhoods in America and attempt to introduce themselves in English when the language in those neighborhoods may indeed be different. Sometimes the only advertising vehicle a company has is language and what is portrayed in the window displays, print advertising, brochures, faxes, or e-mail messages. Thus, your homework on the target language has to be completed prior to sending any message, regardless of how it is delivered.

The Kozy Shack example

Kozy Shack Enterprises, Inc. in Hicksville, New York is a manufacturer of ready-to-eat refrigerated puddings. I met Debra Núñez McWhirter, in charge of international sales for Kozy Shack, at Expo Comida Latina. I listened to her mingle with prospective clients, easily switching between English and Spanish, and beautifully describing the richness of Arroz con Leche and how the product hits home with the Hispanic consumer.

During a follow up phone call, Ms. Núñez McWhirter explained to me that she was raised in Puerto Rico and that she is the only bi-lingual employee in the sales department. She said she is often given the responsibility for product translation. She shared her comical story about the use of the word *preservative* in English and how it is similar, or a cognate, in Spanish, to preservativo. While appropriate and correct in some areas to describe preservative, as in food preservative, in other regions or dialects the term is colloquial for condom.

More important, Ms. Núñez McWhirter also passed along Kozy Shack's experience of trying to sell rice pudding to Hispanics.

"We received little to no play from the Hispanic consumer

when the rice pudding was labeled in English, but when we marketed it as *Arroz con Leche* and better positioned its imagery on the package, the product took off. In essence, there existed no correlation between Latinos and rice pudding. None! Looking back, every Latin American country has an *Arroz con Leche*. *Arroz con Leche* to us Latinos is comfort and creamy and we want to see it in language and in-culture."

Ms. Núñez McWhirter and Kozy Shack recognize the need to communicate in-language on the shelf at the retail level. Kozy Shack supports the success of the overall product (rice pudding) by extending its reach into the Hispanic community as *arroz con leche*.

Kozy Shack has also tuned into a second critical step, producing good, reliable translation. Look for yourself in your local grocery store for the product and you will see colorful vibrant orange packaging representing the Kozy Shack Original Rice Pudding-Original Arroz Con Leche. And as Ms. Núñez McWhirter suggested the relationship between Arroz Con Leche and Hispanics is culturally and linguistically relevant.

Don't ever ignore packaging. Just for the fun of it, walk through a local bodega and look at the colors the bodega uses to draw attention to certain categories or certain areas of the bodega. The same is true for products and their packaging. Some have called packaging the fifth P, right alongside of product, price, place and promotion. Packaging should convey many product attributes, which are best categorized by Dr. Philip Kotler below. Decisions surrounding size, shape, text, brand mark, environmental awareness, safety concerns and color must all be considered in the packaging concept. But most importantly, it must attract positive attention, such as the fine work done at Kozy Shack with their Arroz Con Leche.

An increasing number of products are sold on a self-service basis in super-markets, discount houses, hypermarts, etc. In an average supermarket which stocks 15,000 items, the typical shopper passes 300 items per minute. Given that 53% of all purchases are made on impulse, the effective packaging operates as a "five second commercial." The package must perform many of the sales tasks. It must attract attention, describe the product's features, create consumer confidence, and make a favorable overall impression.

Kozy Shack's successful rice pudding

Kozy Shack's Dulce de Leche. Note the Spanish is listed first on this tasty Carmel pudding

Source: *Marketing Management*, Eighth Edition, Philip Kotler, ©1994 Prentice Hall

Out of touch

All the due diligence spent prior to launch, the segmentation studies, targeting, and positioning will not overcome improper language. Improper product language sends a disrespectful message to customers. While some language slips may be comical in nature, it becomes frustrating to customers when on a return visit to the store or neighborhood; the message has not been removed or repaired.

As retailers and manufacturers you have to ask, "What is the cost to build language and verification of that language into each and every market where my product is available?" If credibility is on your mind, we are speaking the same language.

Checklist for language choice

- What is the definition of U.S. Hispanic for your industry?

- What is the definition of U.S. Hispanic for where you wish to market the product or service from your industry?

- What is the purchasing power of the U.S. Hispanic for your product in the markets you wish to enter?

- How English proficient is your marketplace? (According to some studies, English proficiency may be as high as 75 percent for adults.) As you set out to measure language preference, insure language preference is assessed at home, at work, and at the point of purchase. Language preferences vary at work, home, and by purchase opportunity. Just because someone has a preferred language at home does not suggest he uses or prefers the same language at work or when purchasing.

- Is the context of your message dependent on environment?

- Is the in-language approach the proper method and worth the cash outlay in an environment where 75 of adult customers are English proficient? Will there be a positive return on investment?

Two unique markets

Spanish Dominant	English Dominant
Normally older	Normally younger
May be foreign-born	Born in U.S. or longer time in U.S.
Traditional in nature	Trendy, hip, influencers
Uses predominantly Spanish media	Better educated
Spanish in most places	Spanish in home, English outside home

Properly, effectively, and responsibly conveying the significance of a message when translating from one language (host) to another language (target) is critical to the message being received by the intended audience. Sometimes, there needs to be close adherence to the subject matter, such as in the translation of operating instructions for an appliance. At other times it may require less restricted translation. Certainly the translated message should be tested in each and every market for clarity and understanding, relevance, and significance.

Media consumption, by language

Language preference	All Hispanics	Native-born Hispanics	Foreign-born Hispanics
Predominantly Spanish	38%	9%	55%
Spanish and English Equally	26%	20%	30%
Predominantly English	36%	71%	15%

Source: The Pew Hispanic Center, National Survey of Latinos, 2002

Remember, while some marketing and advertising agencies are in touch with the general market, it does not necessarily mean they are in touch with the Hispanic market, or with the intricacies of language. Often times, what was initiated as an innocent attempt to appeal to this market evolves into a message that is denigrating, stereotypical, embarrassing, and even cumbersome. Taking the proper steps to ensure this does not occur means doing your own research and performing the due diligence on work an outside firm helps you complete.

CHAPTER 9

Crafting a Message That Touches Hispanic Consumers

Retailers who want to attract Hispanic customers usually have limited budgets and little assistance when it comes to tailoring advertising messages. This chapter is designed to help overcome the "message" problem, but not to deal with the "messenger" or the choices of media. Hispanic and multicultural advertising agencies are available at both the national and local levels to help perform this task.[1]

Those who have managed well-known products and brands and faced some uphill battles in their pursuit of the Latino market have some advice to offer about the various messages with which to reach this emerging consumer. In general, all of these individuals have set aside their own general market beliefs in order to become educated to what was once a new consumer to them. Most told me about battles and real world conversations surrounding the funding of these programs. The largest battle of all was the constant desire of management to "just use the same message as the general market."

The first question you have to answer is "Why should I spend the cash to create advertising in Spanish if we can reach the Hispanic consumer in English?

One answer is that advertising in Spanish is more effective

---

1 You can order a directory of members of the Association of Hispanic Advertising Agencies www.ahaa.org.

with more people, even among bilinguals. As the number of U.S. Hispanics grows and this segment gains pride in its culture, interest in the Spanish language is growing as well. The two charts below show that the Spanish language is retaining its popularity, and that advertising in Spanish is enticing to a greater segment of the U.S. Hispanic population.

Spanish language is important to Hispanics

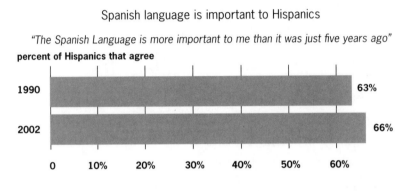

"The Spanish Language is more important to me than it was just five years ago"

percent of Hispanics that agree

1990 — 63%
2002 — 66%

0   10%   20%   30%   40%   50%   60%

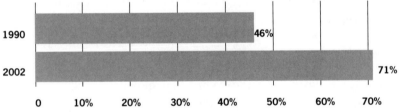

"I would be more inclined to purchase brands which are advertised in Spanish"

percent of Hispanics that agree

1990 — 46%
2002 — 71%

0   10%   20%   30%   40%   50%   60%   70%

Source: Yankelovich Partners 1990 & 2002 Hispanic Monitor Study, as quoted in a presentation by Telemundo

According to a 2002 study by Yankelovich Partners, 60 percent of Hispanics surveyed felt as though they can not understand commercials in English as well as they can understand them in English, and 69 percent agreed with this statement: "I get more information about a product when it's advertised in Spanish than when it's advertised in English only."

The benefits of Spanish-language advertising, as discussed in previous chapters, are subtle but have potentially far-reaching implications. It's a joke for marketers and manufacturers to believe that all Hispanics in the U.S. will eventually become—or even wish to become—so acculturated as to blend completely with the mainstream market. The reality is that we have a juxtaposition of different societies and cultures. It is not about the U.S. Hispanic blending. Rather it is about various races and ethnicities seeking to understand each other.

It's not just language—The National Pork Board (NPB)

In June 2004 I talked with Ceci Snyder, Assistant Vice President of Consumer Marketing for the National Pork Board (NPB), an independent body appointed by the Secretary of the USDA. Ms. Snyder, who has nine years of experience with the NPB, explained the highly successful: "El Cerdo es Bueno," (Pork is Good) campaign, which launched in five markets in 2002.

The National Pork Board's goal: "To strengthen the position of the pork industry and expand markets for pork producers with a key consumer in mind, the U.S. Hispanic."

To reach these consumers, the NPB used Spanish-language television and a public relations campaign. The costs associated with Spanish-language television versus English language television made the Spanish buy cost effective. Readers probably know the tagline, "Pork. The Other White Meat®." However, that general market message did not seem to be culturally adaptable for the Hispanic market. It was produced to capitalize on growing trends of "chicken fatigue" and "burger boredom," which did not seem appropriate for the U.S. Hispanic market. Enter, *El cerdo es bueno.*

In researching the U. S. Hispanic market, The National Pork Board found many trends it liked:

- The population of Hispanics in the U.S. reached 39.3 million in July 2003, accounting for one half of the 9.4 million residents added to the nation's population since Census 2000. Its growth rate of 13 percent since 2000 was almost four times that of the total population, according to the U.S. Census Bureau.

- Whereas the median age in the U.S. population is 35.9 years, the median age for U.S. Hispanics is 26.7 years, again a Census finding.

- U. S. Hispanic households are larger in size, roughly 3.6 people versus 2.6 in the general market, according to the Census.

- U.S. Hispanics are lucrative grocery customers.

- U.S. Hispanics have a different attitude concerning pork than do consumers in the general market.

The attitudinal factor was the impetus behind the *El cerdo es bueno* campaign. The National Pork Board found that U.S. Hispanics were already predisposed to eating pork, with 86 percent being pork consumers. They also believed that pork was "the most delicious" protein and used it as a main ingredient in traditional Hispanic recipes. However, there were also many misperceptions about the product.

Health and safety concerns that originated in their homelands were also found to be concerns in the United States. According to Ms. Snyder, this may be due to poor processing in Latin America, or Latin America suppliers may be using a lower quality hog and the concerns are indeed valid. She explained, "The quality and care of livestock in many Latin American countries is well below U.S. standards, resulting in sickness and the fear of trichinosis. Had it not been for our research and focus groups, we would have not known that these fears, founded in the country of origin, carried over to the U.S. meat counter."

As to the "Pork—The Other White Meat®" campaign designed for the general market, Ms. Snyder said, it would not work because not only did the NPB have to educate the U.S. Hispanic consumer, but it also found that:

- Many U:S. Hispanics believed pork to be a red meat or its own category.

- Food safety and health concerns were much more important than parity with chicken.

- The general market campaign had underscored the need for a different cultural approach.

To make use of the above findings, Ms. Snyder and her team launched the *El cerdo es bueno* advertising campaign in five markets: Chicago, Houston, Los Angeles, Miami, and Phoenix. At a national level, a combination of advertising and public relations was employed.

"We have been able to use credible spokespersons in the media, as well as point of purchase information at supermarkets," she said. "But the large success of the message campaign has been the public relations program consisting of bilingual registered dieticians and a well-known Ph.D. nutritionist."

When asked, "Why not a celebrity?" Ms. Snyder replied, "In focus groups we were told dieticians and nutritionists were preferred and trusted more versus the actor or other celebrity and this may be due to the Hispanics' understanding of culture and credibility with people of authority."

The *El cerdo es bueno* campaign has been so successful that it is now expanding from the five original markets to twelve. The lessons learned from the *El cerdo es bueno* campaign can be applied to any business.

Healthy Cuts of Pork
Cortes Saludables del Cerdo

Chicken breast*
Pechuga de pollo*
0.9g   3.1g

Pork tenderloin*
Filete de cerdo*
1.4g   4.1g

Pork boneless sirloin chop**
Chuleta sirloin**
1.9g   5.7g

Pork boneless loin roast*
Lomo de cerdo*
2.2g   6.1g

Pork boneless top loin chop**
Chuleta de cabeza de lomo**
2.3g   6.6g

Pork loin chop**
Chuleta de lomo**
2.5g   6.9g

Pork boneless sirloin roast*
Sirloin de cerdo*
2.5g   7.0g

Pork rib chop**
Chuleta de costilla**
2.9g   8.3g

Pork boneless rib roast*
Asado de Costillas*
3.0g   8.6g

Chicken thigh*
Muslo de pollo*
2.6g   9.3g

Saturated Fat
Grasa Saturada

Total Fat
Grasa Total

*Roasted, **broiled (Based on 3oz. cooked meat, skinless or trimmed.) Source for pork and chicken data: USDA Handbook 8 Series.

*Asado, **a la parrilla (Basada en 3 onzas de carne cocida, sin piel o con grasa recortada.) Datos del cerdo y pollo tomados del USDA Handbook 8 Series.

pork
Calidad U.S. Pork.™

Its advertising objective was to reach the U.S. Hispanic consumer while focusing on education via safety and nutrition. The message sent was "Pork is good, nutritious, delicious and safe. U.S. pork equals high quality." The campaign used radio, outdoor, and magazine advertising, and public relations using dieticians as spokespeople. There was a microsite on the NPB website in Spanish. Retail promotions included bilingual meat-case signs and recipes.

Many retailers provided positive feedback pertaining to the NPB campaign.

As a result of the campaign, consumers purchased pork more frequently and in larger quantities equaling a 14 percent increase in pork expenditures or about $13 million in incremental pork purchases. One retailer, Food City, a grocer, ran two NPB Hispanic promotions in 2002 and achieved double-digit results in its fresh pork sales as a result of each promotion. Additionally, the Spanish-language radio station that the NPB used reported a five-fold increase in consumer response to the NPB/Food City sweepstakes offerings in comparison with other such promotions.

Using radio with the Hispanic market

The National Pork Board realized that it needed to use Spanish-language media, but that realization doesn't come easily to every organization. Daniel S. Turpin, Senior Account Executive and New Business Development Coordinator for WLEY radio station, 107.9, a member of the Spanish Broadcasting System, told me that his biggest challenge in selling advertising for WLEY is persuading potential advertisers of the strength of the Hispanic market in Chicago.

Mr. Turpin explained: "For whatever reason, despite Chicago's enormous Hispanic population of 1.8 million—close to

20 percent of the entire metropolitan area—there are still a few "out-of-the market" agencies that seem to not want to believe that a Midwestern market such as Chicago could be as viable as Los Angeles, New York, or even Miami.

Mr. Turpin continued, "Another challenge that I continually face from potential Hispanic advertisers is how to handle the creative when considering whether to buy a Hispanic station on a radio campaign. Most of the buying and planning people that I work with have no problem figuring out how to effectively buy a Hispanic radio station for a radio campaign. However, they have no idea how to create an effective radio commercial that appropriately targets the typical Chicago Hispanic. Unfortunately, many general-market ad agencies feel compelled to hire freelancers to create commercials."

As you can see from this example, not everyone is thirsty for this consumer. It is at times an arduous process. Those who get it, get it! Those who don't often outsource creative and end up with *nada*, which creates poor feelings among managers and consumers, ultimately yielding poor sales and lower budgets for advertising.

For some companies, a new campaign may be their first step into the tepid waters of the Hispanic market. As Dan Turpin told me, "Because some of my clients don't know the market, I end up being a consultant as well!"

Advertising agency—the challenge

One way to make sure your agency is up to the challenge of creating a campaign for your Hispanic target market is to consider these non-cost-related questions:

- Does your agency employ specialists who will be able to perform the job better than keeping it internal? Who are these specialists? What are their backgrounds?

- What is the agency's point of view toward solving your problem?

- Is the agency national or local and is it familiar with the local culture and buying habits? Does it understand the differences in buying habits that exist between Cuban Americans in Miami, Mexican Americans in Phoenix, and Spaniards in Boston?

- Does the agency cover all the relevant markets?

- What type of brand image does the company wish to project? Will it be the same as the image projected to the general market?

Align yourself with an agency you trust and an agency that understands the Hispanic space.

Grassroots approach

It is difficult to find consistent and applicable information on customer and employee turnover. Not many companies are willing to publish data on their customer turnover. However, assuming both customer and employee turnover, it is a challenge to send a consistent message to new customers via a new and inexperienced employee. One way to overcome the challenge is to focus on building relationships with customers via a grassroots approach where you bring the voice of the consumer and the complexion of the community into your retail environment.

A very simple example of this is the Mexican supermarket manager on Chicago's near north side indicating he has, "All the Posada needs for the Holiday Season." (We discussed *posada* in chapter three. Whereas most may know Posada as an inn, Posada is also the celebration surrounding the reenactment of the journey of May and Joseph looking for shelter or an inn to give birth to Jesus. This reenactment is recognized in many Hispanic communities and celebrations are planned around it.) This simple message suggests the voice of his community is heard and the complexion of the community is represented in the store.

A grassroots approach should:

- Respect the values of the consumer.

- Recognize what is important to the consumer: food, family, religion, sport, education, and celebration.

- Understand the relevance of celebrations such as Cinco de Mayo or other important dates.

- Be cognizant of how humor is used within culture. An example of this is that Latin American women are more appreciative of humor surrounding their body and the curves associated with them versus the general public woman! Latinos make fun of their own culture, but any attempt at using humor in advertising or marketing should first be discussed with a key group of friendly, known customers.

- Connect with cultural icons. During national heritage days, U.S. Hispanics from around the globe proudly display the colors of their homeland flags. The flags can be seen in front of homes as well as hanging from automobile windows and sunroofs. Walk around any large U.S. city where Hispanics are a substantial share of the market and you will find your potential customer wearing a favorite homeland soccer team jersey, whether it is Chivas, Tecos, or Argentina Futbol Association. This too is connection with a cultural icon.

Dan Turpin at WLEY tells this story of a successful grass roots effort:

One huge success story involves my radio station, WLEY, one of my biggest accounts Pepsi, and the Chicago White Sox. For the past five years, we had always executed a "non-spot" radio program for Pepsi targeted at the very hard-to-reach *supermercados*. "Hard to reach" meant that the soft drink manufacturer did not always best know how to approach this mom-and-pop type of ethnic business.

In a nutshell, we gave these *supermercados* a series of live remote broadcasts that revolved around the theme of "Your Ticket to Enjoyment." At the remotes we distributed Pepsi products and encouraged our listeners to sign up and win a variety of big-ticket items such as a car, motorcycles, or concert tickets. One year we centered everything around the chance to see Shakira, who at that time was the spokesperson for Pepsi, at a very exciting out-of-the market venue. Pepsi and WLEY merchandise, such as tee shirts and key chains, was available and it was just a very fun and fantastic environment!

Last year we decided to tie in baseball. The Mexican and Puerto Rican Americans identified to us their cultural tie to baseball. Pepsi Chicago, WLEY, and the Major League Chicago White Sox collectively decided to enhance the program by including the White Sox as a third-party participant.

We will be conducting a series of remotes again, not only at the *supermercados*, but also at U.S. Cellular Field (Sox Park), giving away skyboxes, White Sox merchandise, and using player appearances at designated WLEY events.

We were thrilled to add to the program! Pepsi loves the program because at a local level Pepsi managers feel they are attracting the Hispanic community and are more in touch with that community. The Chicago White Sox executives are ecstatic because they found a way to tap into Chicago's massive Hispanic market, not to mention that the timing is perfect because the Sox have a new Hispanic manager, Ozzie Guillen.

The above example is grassroots. It ties together celebration, music, sport, and cultural icons such as Shakira and one you may not know but Hispanic baseball fans know, Ozzie Guillen!

Direct marketing

Chapter 8 included questions you may want to ask before deciding whether to advertise in Spanish or English. Whatever that decision, you still have to reach out to your customers in the most cost-effective way. Fortunately, a wide variety of vehicles including traditional media are available targeted especially to Hispanics.

For example, a study by New California Media, an association of ethnic media organizations found that 84 percent of California's three largest minority groups can be reached by ethnic media. Sergio Bendixen, President of Bendixen & Associates, which carried out the study, reported that 51 percent of Hispanics preferred Spanish-language radio stations, 43 percent preferred ethnic television networks, stations, and programs; and 23 percent preferred ethnic newspapers.

But advertising loyalty is only as strong as the vehicle used to reach the consumer, so ensure that your ad is placed where it will make it into the hands and minds of your customers. As to why that is so important, consider a number of key points about your Hispanic customer not yet mentioned.

Because the Hispanic population is spreading across the nation while their buying power and their use of credit cards is increasing, many companies are marketing to Hispanics via direct mail. Many direct marketers are finding that Hispanics love direct mail. They consider direct mail to be new and exciting. No language barrier exists while reading at home. It is less intimidating, decision-making can be a family process, and it is comfortable. As immigration continues so will the audience base for direct marketing and as your customers acculturate, your direct marketing message should follow them up the acculturation ladder.

The internet

The online medium is central to Hispanics' lives and a number of companies realize this. One example is Southwest Airlines, which devotes an entire page and sub pages to its Spanish-preferred customer titled, "Bienvenidos a southwest.com!" Today, the first impression your company makes on a consumer is often your website. Thus with simply a click, your customer may decide whether to do business with you.

According to Lee Vann, Principal of the Captura Group, the Hispanic market has reached critical mass. As of January 2004, 13 million U.S. Hispanics were online, which represented the largest Hispanic population online anywhere. Many Hispanics online are upscale and new online recruits are outpacing the general market. Place on top of those statistics the fact that the Hispanic internet user is younger than the general market and the Hispanic internet initiative may not be that difficult a sell to your IT group. But how do you analyze this opportunity? Or what major retailers can you cite in an effort to substantiate your decision? The obvious is AOL Latino. The not-so-obvious is Sears enespanol.com.

Analyzing the opportunity should be no different than any other capital investment in your portfolio. Your Hispanic internet initiative should also have approval, support, or a champion from the top of your company. This champion should oversee the multicultural marketing initiative and help determine the profit potential associated with your initiative, as well as determining the potential risk associated with it. Return on Investment for your Hispanic internet initiative should compliment your overall portfolio.

Some final thoughts

Whether you are building a national advertising effort such as the National Pork Board, a local effort such as WLEY and Pepsi in Chicago, or a store effort such as the grocer on Chicago's north side, what are the next steps?

- Continue to expand your knowledge of the Hispanic customer.
- Refine and modify your approach based on new knowledge and changing customer demands.
- Like the National Pork Board, expand the program into sensible markets.
- Clearly define your mission.
- Seek out internal support and familiarize everyone in your company with your Hispanic advertising efforts.
- Conduct the necessary research to reach the customer and minimize risk.
- Select the proper partner with the expertise required.
- Develop a culturally relevant and receptive program.
- Don't hesitate to refine and fine tune as you learn more about the market.

CHAPTER 10

Dance to the Salsa!

The concept of Hispanic marketing or multicultural marketing is not a fad or a trend. It is a viable movement, which is sweeping across America and its taste and flavor add to America!

Take this scene as an example: In Chicago throughout many neighborhoods, *Paleteros* peddle their three wheel bikes with a refrigerated box carrying *Paleta* (ice cream) in the flavors of Coco, Piña, Fresa, and Naranja, up and down the streets. Along with ice cream, they are selling part of the culture. The different cultural place of ice cream among Americans and U.S. Hispanics is a good example of the ways cultural differences exist in our marketplace.

As an American consumer, I view my Ben and Jerry's ice cream as an indulgence, a guilty pleasure. I occasionally find myself hoarding the Ben and Jerry's for myself, actually hiding it towards the rear of the freezer so no one else will notice it.

However, among my soccer friends on the north side of Chicago who enjoy ice cream, it is not uncommon to see grown men abandon their game of soccer to enjoy a frozen and fruited selection on a four-inch wooden stick. I am certain the rapidly melting frozen delight is the major attraction, but so is the opportunity for conversation; an opportunity to reconnect to those selling and to those buying. Commonplace conversations revolve around villages, last names, and where in the city one now resides. Another topic is the quality of the *paleta*. To some, it is too creamy; to others, it is not creamy enough, while to others, there is not enough fruit.

Many who peddle are veterans and have peddled the streets in Mexico. The *paleteros* know exactly when to ring-a-ling, ring the bicycle bell. They know that in certain neighborhoods, the hottest-selling offering is the *Arcoiris*, or rainbow of flavors, and they know when school dismisses and the mass schedule in my neighborhood on Sunday.

These *paleta* companies are not only appealing to taste created in the homeland, but also to the conversation ice cream invokes. General market supermarkets and ice cream vendors like Baskin Robbins and Dairy Queen don't meet this need.

As to the producers of the *paletas*, it is about customizing the flavors to the taste of the home turf and being in the right place at the right time. Many Mexicans prefer guava and mango while customers with origins in the Caribbean prefer pineapple and coconut, while still other customers from other parts of the globe may prefer citrus flavors, or green tea, and red bean flavors.

Selling ice cream to U.S. Hispanic consumers is a lesson in understanding the conversation surrounding ice cream. For these Hispanics, ice cream is not an indulgence or a guilty pleasure. Ice cream is communal and available to the entire family and friends of the family. It drives conversation and community. For the *paleteros* it is about being in the right place at the right time and satisfying needs.

Take advantage of being in the right place at the right time

In spite of all your good intentions to listen and learn, barriers will exist. For most people, nothing worth having is easy and the barriers, which may have been created by previous management styles, may need to be removed or replaced, but you are in the right place at the right time and you possess the talent and the resources to initiate a successful program.

I believe that owners and operators of independent stores are the backbone and shoulders for this movement. Many of them arrived in the U.S. with nothing other than a dream, strong shoulders, and loving and supportive families. These same families are the men who 30 years ago pushed push carts through the streets of Brooklyn sharpening knives and delivering milk and dairy to Cuban and Puerto Rican families. At the end of the day, the children of these same families pulled their red wagons to the corner store to fulfill Mom's needs for dinner that night. It was about community.

Today these kids are living across the globe and one such kid, Dennis De La Mata, now a 52-year-old Cuban-Spanish American living in Chicago, proudly supports his heritage by still shopping at neighborhood bodegas for specialty cuts of meat and cheeses. Like his childhood in Brooklyn, it is about connection and community and giving back to the community, similar to the way he did as a child. It is about taking care of those who take care of me, who give me the special treatment, and who can talk to me in Spanish.

We speak of moving outside of the U.S. to find new markets for our products. While certainly this is fundamental business practice, so too is attracting different and new in-country consumers to our products or to our stores in our own community. The global culture exists here in our backyard. It is our job to "unpack" it!

Unpacking the global culture means allowing these consumers to stay awhile and to invite them in as our guests. Understanding them allows them to unpack their belongings and become part of our communities, participating in our neighborhoods.

The local "global" culture and the unpacking of it will

require special language skills and it will necessitate understanding ethnic and social and religious differences, but these are the characteristics on which our country was built. It is worth the trip through your own neighborhood. Is it worth varying a strategy in order to earn these important and loyal customers.

Whether you merchandise a new store, recognize a culture modifier, realize code switching is the proper language concept to implement, or merely market to this consumer in a Spanish-language newspaper, you will be participating in one of the greatest consumer movements of modern time.

Break the culture barrier and learn more about high context and low context cultures and the next time you are at a coffee shop or corner store or gas station, look around and watch the theater that is occurring around you, similar to the theater at Marlins en Miami, mentioned in the opening chapters.

The Hispanic marketplace has reached a critical mass and the time to act is now. It is the crescendo of the movement and to be successful we must move from marketing in Spanish to marketing in-culture to U.S. Hispanics. Take the time, gather the resources, establish the team, then find a champion for the project, but don't sit on the side and watch. Instead, dance the salsa, eat a jalapeño, sip a sip of *horchata*, or have an original Cuban sandwich underneath a palm tree in the heat of a Miami summer. Become passionate about your part in this. Leave a better business for those that will follow. Allow this consumer movement to be present at your place of business. As representatives of the U.S. culture it is our opportunity to appropriately express our authenticity and our uniqueness to those around us and to this consumer. Many will lead and some will follow. Regardless of your place in this movement, you too can be part of positive and lucrative change.

Strong Sales and *Paz* (Peace).

Index

About the Author

JIM PERKINS spent 15 years in the corporate world prior to founding his own business, ÚLATAM Solutions Group, a firm which helps organizations build a Hispanic offering for their retail unit. While with ExxonMobil Corporation and 7-Eleven of México, S.A. de C.V., Mr. Perkins marketed to various cultures in a number of cities. But it was on the streets of Miami; Los Angeles; Chicago; Monterrey, Mexico; Caracas, Venezuela and Seville, Spain that he learned to better build a retail unit in which all are welcome and the product desired is available.

Mr. Perkins has written articles on topics ranging from language acceptance, to confection preferences of Latinos, to tobacco and Latinos. He currently guest lectures to universities and business and often suggests to his audience, "This Latino explosion is not coincidence, if you have not started you may be somewhat behind!"

Mr. Perkins started studying Spanish at the age of 11 and is a student of the Spanish language and Latin Cultures. A graduate of Purdue University and current student at the University of California at Berkeley, Mr. Perkins applies time spent in Spain, México, South America and the Caribbean as well as his education, to his study and analysis of the multicultural marketing space.

Mr. Perkins currently lives in Chicago, Illinois, where he can be reached at: 312-952-0963 or at www.ulatam.com